W9-BET-327

CECILIA M. WATSON

Pacific Press Publishing Association
Boise, Idaho
Montemorelos, Nuevo Leon, Mexico
Oshawa, Ontario, Canada

Edited by Lawrence Maxwell
Cover by Tim Larson
Cover Photo by Robert Dawson
Type set in 10/12 Century Schoolbook

Copyright © 1986 by
Pacific Press Publishing Association
Printed in United States of America
All Rights Reserved

Library of Congress Cataloging in Publication Data

Watson, Cecilia M.
  Spiritfruit: God's buffet of Christian graces.

  Bibliography: p.
  1. Spiritual life—Seventh-Day Adventist authors.
I. Title. II. Title: Spirit fruit.
BV4501.2.W3765   1986   248.4'86732   85-25810
ISBN 0-8163-0628-1

86 87 88 89 ● 6 5 4 3 2 1

Contents

Synopsis

The gifts of the Spirit as found in Galatians 5 are like a great kaleidoscope of love, a rainbow cast from a crystal prism. They become a vivid spectrum of color when the Light of Life shines through them.

Spiritfruit is about commoners and monarchy, saints and sinners, the ancient and the very modern. While viewing them in the great mirror of time, we see ourselves as well. The best examples are notable trailblazers whose thoughts and actions influenced others for centuries. The worst remain as graphic examples of danger and destruction. They either triumphed by faith or perished along the road to the Promised Land through disobedience and unbelief.

The subject of the most important desires of the human heart are discussed in Chapter 1: To love and be loved, to be recognized individually, to stay young in heart, to be creative and productive, and to have a purpose in life. Chapter 2 deals with joy and inner happiness through Christ. Finding your own special quiet time where peace overcomes chaos, worry, and the anxieties of life is discussed in Chapter 3. Chapter 4 shows why we need patience in every corner of our lives. Chapter 5 contrasts kindness and various forms of abuse in society—physical, verbal, and emotional. Chapter 6 describes goodness through creative Christian living. Chapter 7 enlarges on faith and the faithfulness of the remnant church. Chapter 8 tells how we can be God's gentle people by allowing Him to lead us. Chapter 9 encourages trailblazers and goal setters to live a Christian life which is constantly moving and growing—to leave the ordinary behind and seek the extraordinary through Christ.

The book is written for Christians who are journeying alone-together to the Promised Land. It is a book of hope and hardship, battles lost and victories won, crushing disappointments and fulfilled dreams.

But most of all, it is about love's ultimate victory through Jesus Christ.

LOVE: Love's Kaleidoscope

From the Christian standpoint, love is power.
—Ellen G. White

When I was a child, someone gave me a kaleidoscope. It was a cylindrical toy similar to a small hand-held telescope. It contained within its inner chamber three mirrors and many small bits of broken, colored glass. When the aperture on one end was held to the eye and the cylinder revolved, the fragments of glass fell into exquisitely beautiful patterns reflected by the mirrors. The more the bits were shaken up, the lovelier the patterns became. So it is in the Christian life; dozens of brightly colored fragments create one whole magnificent design.

Just when we think we know everything about love, someone comes along and presents a new idea or shakes the pieces into a unique pattern, and we discover an entirely different dimension of love's beauty. The kaleidoscope rolls, and we behold yet another facet of love's wonder. The last word on love will never be written, because it is as infinite as is God who created it. This book is a study of the love that brings joy, peace, patience, kindness, goodness, faithfulness, gentleness, and self-control into every aspect of the Christian life.

One of the most important desires in the human heart is to love and be loved. This love involves more than sharing an income, dividing the chores, or deciding who takes care of the children. It means a commitment and a willingness to act responsibly for the lives of others. It means total involvement. Love is the strongest motivating force in life. It is known to be so powerful that it has taken individuals beyond the point of

7

self-preservation to self-sacrifice. This is timeless love, able to endure hardship and deny self for the sake of others. While all the world seeks for riches and power, a Christian realizes that love is the greatest treasure on earth. Love is sharing with another. It is centered on giving. It is an emotion that did not originate with man but was set in his heart at the beginning.

It is not the love of power but the power of love that brings about effective influence in the world, in the community, in the church, and in the home. Love is not merely an outpouring of emotion; it is a deep, abiding principle. While an absence of love leads to corruption and the cultivation of destructive habits, true love brings forth goodness, happiness, and peace. The unique miracle of love is that it can conquer evil and hatred without being destroyed. Although it can be shared over and over, the supply never diminishes. The more we give, the more we are given in return. It is love that survives when all else fails, because the Source is infinite and inexhaustible. "God *is* love." 1 John 4:16, emphasis supplied.

June Strong says, "The greatest happinesses of my life sprang from those moments when love forced itself beyond the barriers in my heart."[1] While love is a source of inestimable delight, its absence can be a source of physical and emotional pain. Psychologically, the unloved individual may manifest any number of bizarre behavioral patterns or personality disorders from infancy through adulthood. We are taught to love, to hate, to envy, to be strong, to survive. We carry these lessons etched in shallow grooves on gray matter for our entire lives. The grooves become furrows with the passage of time, and the experiences of life continue to cut deepest in those areas which are cultivated most often. So it is that the smiling or troubled child lives on in the carefree or neurotic adult. "We need others. We need others to love and we need to be loved by them. There is no doubt that without it, we too, like the infant left alone, would cease to grow, cease to develop, choose madness and even death."[2]

Christ's words and actions had convincing power because they came from a heart filled with love and compassion for others. This unselfish love proved itself to be genuine as it has continued to flow through twenty centuries of believers. "Without the spirit of love, no one can be like Christ. With this living principle in the soul, no one can be like the world."[3] If there is a faulty connection between the human heart and the real Source of love's power, and unless we continually connect with that Source, we burn out. "God is love, and love is life."[4]

What heartaches, suffering, and grief we would avoid if we would only learn to put God first. Isn't it amazing how we persist in pushing great boulders of fear, guilt, hurt, and worry uphill by ourselves! What a fierce struggle for nothing! Anne Ortlund says, "Work out the implications in your own life of putting God first."[5] Make Him first, last, and best in everything you do. What a joy, an ecstatic joy, when we finally learn this most difficult lesson!

"God loves you," the old man shouted as I walked past. In fact, he yelled it very loudly to anyone within earshot that warm summer day in the downtown mall. I smiled in his direction and kept walking. I noticed several others chuckling at him. He was feeding the pigeons near the fountain, and I mused that he was trying to scatter the gospel as he was the popcorn. I did my shopping and headed back to the car. "God loves you," he proclaimed again as I passed. I turned and said, "I know He does." And then I added, "The question is, Do we love God?" He stared at me incredulously. I smiled and walked on.

Over the past several years, the fact that God loves humanity has been advertised on everything from T-shirts to flashing neon lights. "Smile, God loves you." Every Christian on earth knows it by heart and hopes the rest of the world will discover it before it's too late. But the great question worth eternity is, Do we love Him? And if we do, what are we doing about it?

The second strongest desire of the human heart is to be recognized as an individual. Even if the contribution we make in our little corner of the world is small, we all love recognition. As noble as it may sound, few people are content to be the silent figure in the shadow of another human being. Standing in the shadowy darkness can be cold and lonely. Our talents are what make us unique and outstanding, and it is only natural that we wish to be recognized because of them. This feeling is present in every heart from six to ninety-six. The school-age child looks eagerly to parents and teachers for acceptance and recognition. A father longs for appreciation from his family for all his hard work. Grandma likes to know that her homemade pies are the best at the church supper. Recognition, affirmation, appreciation, and acceptance are among our strongest desires. We love to be loved just for ourselves.

Our third desire is to look as young as we feel. (And you thought you were the only one!) Cosmetics companies, sports-equipment dealers, and the food industry have capitalized on this theme for years. We are assured that their particular brand of beauty cream, muscle builder, or health food will make us attractive and younger looking. We live in a youth-oriented society.

The reason millions of people spend billions of dollars on these and other products every year is that they are trying (sometimes desperately) to preserve what they have, or they are trying to regain what they have lost. They exercise, go on crash diets, and buy the latest fashions because of a burning desire on the inside to look youthful on the outside. Christians are not ignorant or free of this desire. Perhaps it is even stronger in us, because we feel we should attest to God's wonderful care of His children. We are His representatives to a dying world. "While we are to guard against needless adornment and display, we are in no case to be careless and indifferent in regard to outward appearance."[6] If we don't present ourselves at our very best, aren't we falling short of the mark? How we dress, walk, talk, and act has an immediate impact on people we meet each day. Surely not one of us would want to unfavorably impress another individual. I am not saying that we should look as if we had just stepped out of the pages of some high-fashion magazine, but the majority of us can afford suitable clothing and a fragrant bar of soap. Never underestimate the power of your appearance. Catherine Booth said, "As I advanced in religious experience I became more and more convinced that my appearance ought to be such as to show everybody with whom I came in contact that I have renounced the pomp and vanities of the world, and that I belonged to Christ."[7]

Researchers have investigated the human experience involved in the first four minutes of contact between individuals. According to studies on the subject, whether you build or break your relationship with strangers, friends, or loved ones depends entirely on those first four minutes. The typical city dweller comes in contact with more people in one year than our nineteenth-century ancestors met in a lifetime.[8] That fact alone offers an exciting challenge to the Seventh-day Adventist Christian. In a world divided by cultural, economic, and racial barriers, consider the power and influence of the first contact. When we present a smiling face, self-confidence, sensitivity to the other person's feelings and problems, and a pleasant appearance we succeed in making a positive contact. The first four minutes may be all the time we have, and it could make a lifetime of difference. Think of the importance of Esther's first four minutes before the king. The future of an entire nation rested on her shoulders when she walked into the chamber room that evening. She had prepared for her mission for over a year, and it would not have been acceptable if she had sauntered in looking disheveled and smelling like a stale washcloth. She, too, needed to attest to God's wonderful care of His children. See Esther 2:12.

There is an art gallery in San Francisco's Ghirardelli Square that is filled with sculptures, ornate wall hangings, cantilevered fountains, and other artistic wonders created to delight the eye. Off in one corner of the room, protected from harm, is a creation of extraordinary beauty. It is a tiny, spun-crystal spiderweb hung with dewdrops that shimmer like diamonds. A defect or scratch on anything else in the gallery might go unnoticed even to the educated eye, but the transparent glass spiderweb demands perfection. It has been draped with precision across a tiny tree limb. The clarity of the crystal is a masterpiece: perfect, fragile, elegant. Crystal perfection.

When we come down to the final analysis of comparison of lives, it is those who are crystal clear and unadorned who are admired most highly. The true elegance of any person lies in the perfection of a beautiful character. It is the uncluttered, the unpretentious, and the unaffected who stand out most brilliantly in the gallery of life.

The fourth aspect of love that dwells in every heart is the wish to be creative. From the small child who scribbles a crayon picture for mother, to the aged grandfather working in his garden, there is a love within us to create something with our own hands. Something that is uniquely "us." Something that says, "I am giving a part of myself to you." It may be a paint-by-number set from the store, but the pride is pure Rembrandt. The hem may be a bit crooked, but there is a sense of accomplishment when the dress is finished. The musician may never perform in Carnegie Hall, but there is great satisfaction in receiving a sincere "amen" at the end of his performance in church. All these things are a gift of love from the heart to someone else.

This brings us to the other side of creative love—a place where all of us can take part. Even if we can't paint, sew, sing, cook, play a musical instrument, or whatever, we can give encouragement to those who do. We all need more encouragement, and we all need to give more to others. Our creativity and the use of our talents is often the direct result of someone else's belief in our ability to succeed. How many people have you encouraged or inspired lately? Are you encouraging others to be all that they can be, or is your influence constantly negative and unhelpful? Are you urging members of your congregation on to greater service in the church and higher goals in life, or are you defeating them with your contentious remarks and negative attitude? Are you an inspiration to your neighbors, or do you avoid them because they may be on the other side of the fence, figuratively or religiously speaking? Do you encourage your spouse to set higher goals? Do your children know they can come to you for help and count on you to support them in any problem or project? And when others inspire you and encourage you, do you act on their support and reach out in faith to greater accomplishments for God?

Isn't church a strange place! We dress up in our finery on Sabbath morning and rush off to church to sit isolated before God. We look good on the outside, we respond positively to the elder at the door, and we give off an air of self-confidence and

total control over the situation. We sit down quietly and en-
gross ourselves in the church bulletin or stare at the back of
someone's head. Inside, our bodies may be broken by disap-
pointment, bruised by adversity, crushed by defeat, and bleed-
ing from sin. There may be a flood of internal hemorrhaging
going on, but we don't let anyone know. After all, they might
judge us less than perfect if we were to admit to any feelings or
hurts. And so we sit there and refuse to reach out or to be
touched by someone else. I have heard people request that
there shouldn't be any visiting between Sabbath School and
church because the sound of conversation might drift into the
main sanctuary and disturb someone. Show me a church that
doesn't visit, and I'll show you a dead church. It is the mingling
of minds, the social contacts, the sharing of lives that stimu-
lates us to service and to love one another. When we are allowed to share our cares and joys, we validate one another as
human beings. I have friends who hug me every week at
church. What a wonderful feeling to know they love me and
care about my life! I don't mean that we should go around hug-
ging everyone we meet—that would be boring and insincere.
But there's nothing quite as warm as a hug to tell someone he
matters to you. We go to church to worship God, of course; but
we should not go there and sit in cold, desperate, lonely isolation. We need to encourage one another. Take a quick look at
Hebrews 10:25, NIV: "Let us not give up meeting together, as
some are in the habit of doing, but let us encourage one another—and all the more as you see the Day approaching."
There is no other feeling that encourages us quite so much as
reaching out in love with a warm smile, a sincere embrace, a
helping hand.

God has seen fit to bless me through the years with a great
number of friends who have encouraged and advised me wisely.
I have also had my fair share of the other type. When I first
began to write, I was excited about an idea I had for a children's
book. I had discussed the possibility with my family and a few
friends. They all encouraged me, except one. "Not a good idea,"
she said. "Won't sell. Too many kids' books on the market
already." My soap-bubble enthusiasm burst with the first jab. I

felt defeated. I shelved my plans for several weeks, until one day another friend dropped by and inquired about the book. She advised me to submit the idea to a publisher and let him decide whether it was worthy or not. She was right, of course. You will never know if your plan or idea will work unless you try. I wrote and rewrote, then submitted the manuscript several months later. The book has sold thousands of copies since the first printing. I am thankful for a friend who believed in me enough to push me toward my goal. It was like a pat on the back or a warm hug. It was an affirmation, a gentle push in the right direction. Love shining through encouragement.

> For all I need live for
> Is this one little minute,
> For life's Here and Now
> And Eternity's in it.[9]

The last aspect of love's kaleidoscope which encompasses every human life is our purpose for being here. A reason to be living. Those who never find that purpose allow themselves to be swallowed up in unhealthful habits, meaningless relationships, sordid lifestyles, false doctrines and religions, and all sorts of foolish pursuits.

Life should be a challenge, not a threat. Those who fail to climb toward greater goals rob themselves of enriching experiences. If they fail to develop their God-given gifts, minds, and relationships to the fullest, they realize somewhere along the line that they have cheated themselves. And ultimately they have cheated God, for they have diminished the opportunity for Him to work through them to love others. God wants us to live up to our greatest potential. That is not a presumptuous statement. I believe He created each one of us for a purpose. He has a plan for you and me. You are where you are at this very moment because you are part of that plan. I am who I am because He made me that way. Knowing that fact, I have found my true purpose for being here. I needn't run around town or around the world trying to find another one.

When James White died in 1881, Ellen did not quit "living."

Instead, she found there was still a purpose for her to go on without him. In place of the bitterness and resentment which she might have felt, she gave only love and created something beautiful for others. She spent the next thirty years caring and giving, and through them all she remained lovable and lovely. No bitter feelings, no regrets, no crankiness, just love. The lack of a spouse did not leave her without goals or a direction in life. She was not half a person because she never remarried. She was a completely whole, vital, sensitive human being. She once said, "Genuine love is a precious attribute of heavenly origin, which increases in fragrance in proportion as it is dispensed to others."[10] Another singularly lovely woman said, "By love I do not mean a vague, aimless sentiment, but a desire for good united with wisdom and fulfilled in word and deed."[11]

Jesus was the greatest liberationist that ever lived. He was a true lover of people and a great advocate of the poor, weak, downtrodden, and abused. People were precious to Him, and He protected their rights and honor. He healed them, talked freely to them, and held individuals in high esteem and beloved friendship. That He cared so deeply and was so sensitive is highly significant. The words He spoke to the woman in the street are filled with power and inspiring love. He helped her up from the dust and said, "Go, and sin no more." John 8:11. His message echoes down through the centuries to us, and we hear, "Go, and change your lifestyle." "Go, and chart new horizons." "Go, and seek higher goals and greater values." "Go, and serve others." "Go, and become all that you can be as a new person in Me." "Go, and love others as I have loved you."

What a challenge! Any one of those commands is reason and purpose enough for living.

We have found that love is many things. It is a desire, a need, a deep longing in every heart. It has never been defined adequately except to say that it is the greatest of all things. See 1 Corinthians 13:13 in most modern versions. It never fits into just one mold, and it never will. The scientist, philosopher, or poet when attempting to define it always appears to be inadequate. The more we find out about love, the more it changes and enlarges. R. D. Laing said, "What we think is less than what we know: What we know is less than what we love: What we love is so much less than what there is; and to this precise extent, we are much less than what we are."[12]

When we consider love in the light of eternity, the possibilities are boundless. Love means opening our arms to life forever. It begins now.

JOY: Joy Is an Inside Job

It is only in sorrow bad weather masters us; in joy we face the storm and defy it.—Amelia Barr (1831-1919)

It has been said that true joy is "Jesus and You with nothing between, J O Y." Another version says that "Joy is Jesus first, Others second, and You last." However it is stated, Jesus is always the essential ingredient in lasting happiness.

Those people who actually walked and talked with Christ while He was on earth found great joy. Mary of Bethany found humble joy sitting at His feet; Lazarus, her brother, found grateful joy in resurrection; the Samaritan woman at the well found unending joy through living water; and Peter found blessed joy in forgiveness. They all discovered happiness because He showed them the secret of tapping deep wellsprings within the soul.

If we hold our hands open to the sunlight, they are filled with its brightness and warmth. When we close them, we capture only darkness and shadows. So it is when we try to find happiness in material things and external pleasures. By seeking to possess and hoard we gain nothing. When we open our hands and hearts in unselfish giving, the joy we already possess is radiated outward.

At times I feel that someone has forgotten to tell Christians to be happy. There are so many who put on a stern face, cold exterior, and unbending will. Where has all the joy gone? "The full-to-overflowing Christian cup is not one that needs to be carried with tensed nerves for fear of spilling a drop! It is full to *overflowing*—the well of His Life is within you, 'springing up to everlasting life.' His idea for us is that we walk naturally, with

17

our eyes on Him, not riveted on our precious cups which He is always filling for us."[1]

One of the most striking examples of a joyful Christian life is found in my neighborhood. "Joy" lives across the street from me. She is an ageless lady; chronologically about seventy—joyously much younger. On warm summer days her front door is always open to the world. She calls out a cheery hello long before you reach the porch steps. Clumps of bright flowers extend greetings along her walk. "How are you today?" "Isn't it a beautiful day?" We fall into comfortable patter. She is eager to hear what my children are doing, how my garden is growing, and how I've been progressing on this book. (She has no idea she is being included.) Interspersed in her conversation are sincere comments like, "I love the flowers I can see in your yard." She smiles readily when the talk is amusing and laughs spontaneously at some of my feeble attempts at humor. Her conversation is sensitive, caring, and genuine.

On either side of her recliner chair, tables are stacked with letters and magazines, the Bible, stationery and pens, and the phone. A long-handled pair of tongs leans against the side of it. Green plants in a white ceramic pot on the end table and daffodils in a nearby vase decorate the room with color and gladness. White kitchen curtains have been carefully ironed, and the sun radiates through them into the cozy nook. But if you see only the things in this home, you will miss the real source of joy.

"Joy" has suffered from rheumatoid arthritis for the past fifteen years. Her hands are knotted, and her fingers are bent and misshapen. She can no longer use them without great pain and difficulty. Dropping a pencil can work an immense hardship on this little lady, who can no longer bend at the waist. Answering or dialing the phone takes painful effort. Her feet are swollen, with huge knots and calluses on every joint. Walking from the living room to the kitchen becomes an excruciating ordeal. But if you look only at the physical characteristics of this woman, you will miss the significant contribution she makes to her little corner of the world.

The obvious question is, Why, in spite of all the pain, does happiness and joy radiate from the woman in the chair? If you ask her about herself, as I have many times, you will soon find yourself talking about something else. She is a master at changing the subject away from her personal troubles. Despite her obviously painful existence, there is no complaining, no crepe-hanging, no doom and gloom. The entire neighborhood beats a path to her door—not to cheer her, but to be cheered by her.

John Milton, in the poem "On His Blindness," wrote, "They also serve who only stand and wait." Surely that must include those who must sit and wait as "Joy" does. She expressed her concern to me one Sabbath afternoon while we were visiting. "What can I do for the Lord when I have to sit in this chair all day? I feel so utterly useless at times." We talked about the difficulties she faces as a chair-bound Christian. I tried to reassure her that her cheerful spirit, loving attitude, and prayerful life were felt by everyone around her; that her influence reached far beyond the walls of her home, far beyond the confines of the old recliner. The love that radiates from her warms an entire city block and some of the world beyond.

She can walk only a few steps every day, but others come from miles around to seek what she freely gives—herself. She spreads happiness around the neighborhood as some people spread honey on cornbread—liberally and freely. Not all sticky and gooey, or dripping down all over, but sweet and pure. Illness, pain, suffering, and hardship cannot separate her (or us) from the JOY of the Lord. The Power that gives her happiness is far greater than a lifetime of infirmity.

The disconcerting opposite example is the joyless Christian who inhabits our ranks. (Or perhaps that is a contradiction in terms—*joyless* and *Christian* don't coexist for long.) We pass these people on the street, we see their grim faces across the aisle at church; they may teach our children, they may even live in our homes. Douglas Cooper in *Living God's Joy* says, "Religion without joy is a counterfeit."[2] Allow me to take that observation one step further—the person who professes to be a follower of Christ but who has no joy in his heart is a counterfeit Christian.

It is possible to be honored for volunteering hundreds of

hours of service at the local hospital or nursing home and never touch another human being by your presence if you fail to share happiness. It is possible to live in a vast metropolis and never share the joy of knowing Christ with a next-door neighbor. It is possible to work with children every day and never show them the delight of having Jesus as their best friend. It is possible to have all your faculties, an alert mind, and a physically active body, and run around town or around the world and never find true joy within yourself. And if the joy within is never discovered, it can never be shared with others. "If I give all I possess to the poor and surrender my body to the flames, but have not love, I gain nothing." 1 Corinthians 13:3, NIV. If I give everything, but fall short of sharing love's joy, I gain nothing.

It was a dreadful day for Lot's wife when she was literally dragged from the cleansing fires of Sodom by two angels. See Genesis 19:16. She had left behind the only things that mattered to her—the comforts, luxuries, and prestige of wealth which she had grown to rely upon. Without the tangibles, she could never enjoy life (at least she thought so), and the thought of leaving them behind caused her to turn for one last, fatal look.

While we may never turn into a salty pillar beside the road, we have all shed enough salt tears to build a gigantic statue, because we have tried desperately to find joy, happiness, and security in things. It is only when we dissolve away all the old, crusty layers of belief in materialistic security that our lives are filled with treasures of far greater value and with happiness which cannot be bought at any price. Joy is an inside job.

Like Lot's wife, many people rush around looking for joy in places, things, and other shallow people. They are recognizable because they are always looking backward over their shoulders at problems, worries, and transient life on earth. They never look forward with anticipation to greater rewards. That's because it is impossible to see where you are going when you are constantly looking behind you.

Joy is like the water from a deep artesian well; an inexhaustible supply springs from deep cisterns once we tap them. Joy flows spontaneously like a bubbling fountain from the heart of the genuine Christian.

It was a hot, dusty, bone-wearying day as the woman plodded along with a water pot perched on her head. Hoping to make the trip quickly and unnoticed, she shuffled as fast as her sandaled feet would permit in the stifling heat. As she drew nearer to the ancient well, she noticed a Jewish traveler reclining against the stones. She ignored him and went straight to the task of drawing water. She was a Samaritan, and Samaritans did not speak to Jews; she was a woman, and women did not speak to men in public; she was a sinner, and her guilt showed. But this man broke the silence with a request. "Will you give me a drink?" Ashamed, she answered with downcast eyes. "How can you ask me for a drink?" And then the conversation changed from well water to living water. He told her of her past and revealed that He was the Messiah she had been waiting for. Weariness, fear, and shame were replaced with spontaneous joy. So much joy, in fact, that she forgot her water jug and ran to tell an entire village of her discovery. See John 4. Centuries later, there are those who are still discovering the living water. With our selective hearts, we can choose to let that joy pour forth from us.

Why not choose JOY!

"I have told you this so that my joy may be in you and that your joy may be complete." John 15:11, NIV.

PEACE: Sanctuary of the Heart

Certain springs are tapped only when we are alone.
—Anne Morrow Lindbergh

In the midst of a holocaust that later stunned the world, two courageous women walked and talked with God in the shadows of a crematorium. Corrie and Betsie ten Boom came face to face with fear and defied it. Cast into Ravensbrück, a concentration camp later known for its cruelty to women during World War II, the two sisters found inner peace and strength to endure great hardships and death. Forced to stand for hours in subzero temperatures and to sleep in lice-infested barracks on wooden boards, these two women fought to stay alive on meager rations and drops from a vitamin bottle. They smuggled a Bible into camp and tore pages from it to give to desperate women starving for spiritual food as well as for physical sustenance.

Corrie described one of their experiences in her book *Tramp for the Lord*. She wrote, "The brilliant early morning stars were our only light. The cold winter air was so clear. We could faintly see the outlines of the barracks, the crematorium, the gas chamber, and the towers where the guards were standing with loaded machine guns. 'Isn't this a bit of heaven!' Betsie had said. 'And, Lord, this is a small foretaste. One day we will see You face-to-face, but thank You that even now You are giving us the joy of walking and talking with You.' Heaven in the midst of hell. Light in the midst of darkness. What a security!"[1] Corrie said that there were three that morning—she, Betsie, and God. Weeks later, Betsie died in camp. But by some miraculous mix-up in papers, Corrie was released. She became an international figure and told her story worldwide. She died on

April 15, 1983, at the age of 91, a gentle, courageous, Christian woman who was a peacemaker for God.

Calm in the midst of chaos. A light at the end of a dark tunnel. Security that is neither physical, social, nor financial, but spiritual. Peace that comes only from God. There are many small irritations, petty frustrations, and annoying experiences that rear their ugly heads every day. And as the circle widens to encompass towns and cities, our nation, our continent, and the entire world beyond, peace seems more and more to be an illusive butterfly rising above human grasp on turbulent currents. It is difficult to find peace amid utter chaos and to escape being upset by things and circumstances that are so often beyond our control. But when a heart is at peace with God, it cannot be made miserable or uncomfortable.[2] "When I turn to Him and expose the problem to Him, allowing Him to see that I have a dilemma, a difficulty, a disagreeable experience beyond my control, He comes to assist. Often a helpful approach is simply to say aloud, 'O Master, this is beyond me—I can't cope with it—it's bugging me—I can't rest—please take over!' "[3]

We may never have to go through the terrifying ordeal that confronted Corrie and Betsie, but we all need their kind of peace to fortify our daily lives. What are you really like deep down inside? Are you all churned up? Is there a tiny time bomb ticking away, waiting to explode when emotions, anxieties, or worries set it off? Or is there a deep, abiding peace which cannot be disturbed or ruffled by externals? Is the butterfly of peace caught securely in your heart's net?

Christ is the only true source of peace in the world, in our homes, in our lives. True peace comes only in receiving Him into our hearts. Without Him security is a fantasy where none of the stories end happily ever after. Jesus said, "Peace I leave with you, my peace I give unto you: not as the world giveth, give I unto you." John 14:27. The peace which "passeth all understanding" (Philippians 4:7) is found in the person of Jesus Christ.

Chaotic, turbulent, unpeaceful homes cause thousands of children and adults to desert them every year. Many run from neglect or abuse into lives of crime, prostitution, and drugs.

Hundreds of others join offbeat, fanatical cults searching for answers, seeking physical love, and wanting to be wanted. Hundreds more seek a permanent solution to the traumas of life by committing suicide. They have been tossed back and forth between uncaring, unloving people to be scattered like autumn leaves by every false teaching and bizarre experiment that blows across the land. Still others are troubled and distracted by the responsibilities and pressures of parenting, and desertion of children is becoming all too commonplace. Stress leads to anger, and anger erupts in the form of child abuse, alcoholism, drug addiction, and other hideous crimes against society. The solid, indivisible nucleus once known as the family is being split by forces that constantly bombard it from within and without.

We live in a world terrified by war, violence, and the threat of nuclear annihilation. The Christian knows that there will never be world peace until Christ comes. But God promised the gift of peace to His followers. "You will keep in perfect peace him whose mind is steadfast, because he trusts in you." Isaiah 26:3, NIV. When we place our hearts and lives in His hands, that perfect peace is ours as a gift. It is called, in the Hebrew language, "shalom." "The Lord gives strength to his people; the Lord blesses his people with peace [shalom]." Psalm 29:11, NIV. It is a peace inside the heart that cannot be touched by externals.

One of the most trite expressions heard today is "Pray about it." We've all had the experience. "My house burned down last week and my boss fired me." Pray about it. "My husband is filing for divorce." Pray about it. "My child has an incurable disease." Better pray about it. Glossy phrases like this are often no more than a pushing aside of reality, an insensitivity to deep emotional pain, or a careless disregard of the anxieties that tend to cripple us. There is certainly nothing wrong in praying about a situation, but prayer in itself is not an answer. It is merely a vehicle by which we obtain answers. Prayer might be compared to a bell that rings in a church steeple or to a fire alarm that goes off at the station—God never ignores such requests for His attention. What praying does for us is to bring our strict attention to focus on God. Through this tender bond we find answers, strength, and courage to overcome. The answer may lie in changing attitudes, the advice of a close friend, or tangible help. Someone has said that worries grind in the grist mill of the mind until they pulverize our peace. Renewed strength and peace of heart and mind return when someone genuinely cares and gives us a human arm to hang on to.

Fears and worries, the inability to cope, and excessive demands made by job and home make up the bulk of the reasons causing modern problems. "Many people are ill not because of something they have eaten, but because of something eating them."[4] In many of her books, Ellen White discussed distress and distressed persons. Over the last century, the first syllable has been dropped from the word, and it has come to be called "stress." Stress, like burnout, seems to be an accepted phenomenon of the 1980s. While our ancestors worried about starvation, freezing to death, or being eaten by wild animals, we worry about fatal diseases, accidents, and nuclear wars. And let's not forget the great obsession we have with money and aging. Recent studies at the University of California at Berkeley found that young people have a great fear of nuclear war. Researchers are concerned that this gnawing fear may be one source of the increase in youth violence, suicide, and disaffiliated behavior such as the bizarre types of "punk" lifestyle. Surveys have found that many students twelve to eighteen years of age feel they would rather die than survive a nuclear war.[5]

One of the greatest contributors to worry, stress, and lack of peace in our lives is our inability to attain unrealistic goals which we set for ourselves. There is a feeling of inadequacy when we fall short of an unreachable mark. This seems to be especially true for Christians, and Adventists are not exempt. We tend to set high standards, and when they are not achieved, we feel guilty. There is often a temptation at this point to give up completely, even to the point of dropping religion entirely. The young woman who starts college and withdraws to get married, may years later feel frustrated and resentful toward her family for "ruining" her life or career. The teacher who climbs the ladder of academic achievement with his eye on an administrative position only to be outpaced by someone younger or more qualified may feel defeated and angry. The executive who sets his heart on becoming vice-president of the company only to have that position handed to a junior officer may feel the bottom has dropped out of his life. We're discovering that women are beginning to suffer in this area as much as men. "As more and more women move into these roles [professional and executive], it is already evident that they will begin to suffer the same consequences as men, in terms of ulcers and coronary problems."[6]

So how do we begin to cope with the stressful situations we encounter every day—whether in the home or on the job? If there were simple answers to this question, we would have known them long ago, and there would be no need for pastors and counselors or for marriage-encounter seminars at secluded mountain retreats. Unfortunately, an answer in twenty words or less does not exist. There are some helpful hints around, however. For instance, when stress is temporary, as when it is caused by family demands, work load, or school exams, time may be the secret remedy. Time alters situations and changes circumstances, often alleviating problems. It may be helpful to put off things until tomorrow. Another day may shed new light on the subject, and from an entirely different angle. Convince yourself that nothing is going to rob you of your peace of mind today. Granted, this is a neat trick if you can manage to do it successfully. And although I have already said that just praying about something is not always the miraculous panacea we wish it were, try saying aloud, "Lord, this problem is too big for me to handle, and I'm going to leave it in Your capable hands." As rhetorical as that may sound, it can be altogether effective. Try it the next time your world starts to unravel around the edges.

When the problem has been one with a longstanding history of recurring strife and trouble (divorce, unemployment, chronic illness, etc.), perhaps a short trip or vacation may ease the tension. The problem will not go away, but often the view from the top of the mountain is quite different from the one you saw standing knee-deep in the trenches. Getting away from it all can be as refreshing as washing your face in a glacier-fed stream.

Physical activity is another proven method of tension relief. Unlike overeating or excessive smoking or drinking, exercise relaxes without causing physical damage or related disease. When you are actively involved in physical sports or exercise, or in helping others in a service-oriented project, your mind is diverted from personal problems. See *The Ministry of Healing*, pages 239, 240. When we stomp out the spiders of stress, the cobwebs that have entangled us are no longer produced. Many times, merely a diversion from one activity to another is more relaxing than complete rest. A walk in the park can soothe the frustrations of a mother who has spent a rainy day indoors or the man who has spent long hours in a hectic office. Some people refer to themselves as "vending machines." All day long, demands are made on them by other people until they feel they have been punched, pulled, and pounded like a vending machine. "Do this!" "Fix that!" "Go there!" "Wait here!" "Stand up!" "Sit down!" Is it any wonder that some of us have been known to get into the car and drive for a hundred miles with no real destination in mind!

The classic biblical example of a worrier constantly robbing herself of peace was Martha of Bethany. She and her sister, Mary, were close friends of Christ and His disciples. See Luke 10:38-42. We are told that "she [Martha] needed less anxiety for the things which pass away, and more for those things which endure forever."[7] When her brother, Lazarus, died, Martha showed exceptional faith and confidence in Christ's power over sickness and death, but she exhibited her usual tension and unrest when she said, "If you had been here, my brother would not have died." John 11:21, NIV.

Martha represents all of us who become distracted and worried with duties and chores. She is the sister to all who feel they are left to do things alone. She typifies those who worry about what others may think. What the church needs is a happy combination of Martha and Mary—the doer and the thinker, the practical and the spiritual, the energetic and the contented. There is a great need for those who eagerly learn at the feet of the Master and then go forth with determination and love to a needy world.

The number one curse of worry is that it keeps us from enjoying life and the things we already have. Martha's worry about food kept her from enjoying Christ's presence in her home. See Luke 10:40. When we are worried about things that could happen in the world such as total global war, terrorism, famine, or whatever, we rob ourselves of happiness. Worry steals valuable time and energy. If we constantly fret about what we are wearing or the lack of it, the stock in our pantry or our stock on Wall Street, the size of our bank account or the size of someone else's, we won't have time to appreciate what we own. When we become occupied with worrying about anything, no matter how important it may seem at the time, we forget to be thankful for what we have.

Jesus tells us in Matthew 6:26, NIV, to look up and learn a valuable lesson from the birds. "Are you not much more valuable than they?" God takes care of His creatures; why are we concerned that He may forget us? There is evidence that poor Martha was the Mother Hubbard type. Although there were no children in the home, she had apparently programmed herself to be a supersister to Lazarus and Mary (whether they needed one or not). It is easy to conclude that she cared for their every need, and that when Mary decided to take a break, poor ole Martha felt victimized. We can hear her muttering to herself, "I do so much for them. No one appreciates all the trouble I go to around here. Mumble mumble. Someday they will be sorry; just wait and see." She gave and gave of herself, sacrificing her own needs and collecting resentment as she went. And like Mother Hubbard of storybook fame, her cupboard finally became bare. She exhausted her supply of peace and patience because she let minor irritations creep in. She forgot this very important thing—she forgot to restock the cupboard.

Worry's second curse is that it makes us feel worthless and forgotten. Worry causes us to forget our worth in God's eyes. We begin to fret and wonder where the next meal is coming from or how we are going to pay the academy bill or what to do if some catastrophe should destroy our home. We begin to doubt God's Word and His ability to care for us, and with that doubt come fear and anxiety. We forget the most important fact of all—He took care of our greatest need at the cross. Perhaps we should write that sentence down and tape it to a bulletin board or the refrigerator door, where all very important messages are kept. Surely He can take care of all our other needs for the rest of our lives.

In talking to Christian friends, I find much worry caused by guilt. Guilt seems to descend like a black cloud around some people, and at times their depression is very difficult to shake. Some say, "If only I hadn't married a nonbeliever." the implication seems to be that life would somehow be perfect and carefree for them if they were married to a fellow believer. Others say, "If only I had finished college, I would have a better job." This statement is often an excuse for not taking advantage of current opportunities. "If we had only sent the kids to church school, perhaps they would be in the church today." This statement usually doesn't consider the fact that all children are imperfect and willful, just as we adults who have God's perfect counsel still choose to go astray. Guilt is a classic form of indulgence in self-pity. We want to be perfect, and we want our kids to live perfect lives. We begin to feel guilty because we believe we are totally responsible for their actions. We all wish we could go back twenty years and start over.

Perfection bothers me. There was only one perfect One, only One who never sinned or made a mistake. We are all responsible for our own wrongs, and that includes our children, who are as imperfect as we are. We need to learn to stop indulging in guilt that has been around for decades. We need to drop it at the foot of the cross with the rest of our heartaches and worries on the monstrous pile which has grown there since Eden. Worry caused by guilt gives us a distorted view of the world and of God and our relationship to Him. It erases God's promises from our hearts, and it becomes very difficult for us to remember any good thing that has happened. "Cut off from God, we are a million raw nerve ends screaming into the blackness."[8]

Jesus says, "Do not worry about tomorrow, for tomorrow will

worry about itself. Each day has enough trouble of its own."
Matthew 6:34, NIV. Some yesterdays are best forgotten; today
must be lived now; all our tomorrows belong to God. "Many
worry and work, contrive and plan, fearing they may suffer
need. They cannot afford time to pray or to attend religious
meetings and, in their care for themselves, leave no chance for
God to care for them. And the Lord does not do much for them,
for they give Him no opportunity. They do too much for themselves, and believe and trust in God too little."[9]

The answer to the peace problem in your life and mine lies in
God's great gift through Christ. "Do not be anxious about anything, but in everything, by prayer and petition, with thanks-
giving, present your requests to God. And the peace of God,
which transcends all understanding, will guard your hearts
and your minds in Christ Jesus." Philippians 4:6, 7, NIV.

Adam had the beautiful garden, Abraham lived beneath the
trees of Mamre at Hebron, and Mary, the mother of Jesus, en-
joyed the serene, quiet hillsides of Galilee. See Genesis 2:8;
13:18; Luke 1:26, 27. How much more we today need a private,
quiet place to draw aside from the pressures of modern life, a
place to retreat from the activities and obligations which tend
to drain us dry. More often than not, there is no time between
the morning news and the late night show to commune with
God or study His Word. During the day, there is scarcely time
to retreat from demanding obligations, the blare of sirens, deaf-
ening music, and boisterous crowds.

In her book *Gift From the Sea* Anne Morrow Lindbergh describes the multiplicity and fragmentation of lives and empha-
sizes the need to strive for simplification.[10] She found solace on
an isolated island for several weeks and while there in a hut
wrote the book which has sold millions of copies. It is not a religious book, but it is quite spiritual and inspirational. She describes her surroundings thus: "Rollers on the beach, wind in
the pines, the slow flapping of herons across sand dunes, drown
out the hectic rhythms of city and suburb, time tables and
schedules."[11] Understandably, she never disclosed the location
of her secret hiding place.

You may never be able to escape to an enchanted island or

take *A Little Journey* along the Maine coastline as June Strong did, but you need time by yourself whoever you are. You may need to hide in the attic or in a corner of your office or on an old park bench. Wherever the place, go there regularly to refresh and refill. "Sanctuary is where you find it. You can find it where you are, in your town, on your street, in your own heart."[12] If you have time to watch television, go shopping, or do whatever else you deem highly important, then you have time to be alone. The sun won't stop shining, the earth won't stop spinning, and there won't even be a worldwide shortage of Christians if you don't find a peaceful sanctuary. But it will certainly be to your benefit if you do.

I have a special place I go when I need to refill and refresh. When life presses in and I need a place to meditate, relax, or reflect, I turn homeward. The old homestead exists today much as it did when I was a child. Over 200 acres of forests, streams, meadows, and orchards are where I left them twenty years ago. Wildlife and wildflowers grow there in abundance. The trees in the apple orchard are rugged, and the branches are gnarled; they stand as silent witnesses to the storms they have weathered. In the springtime, blossoms seem to appear overnight as if by magic. Buds are one day swollen and tight, the next they open, delicate with perfume. A warm rain can give them birth. For the sheer joy of it, I can still climb among the branches and fill my senses with the fragrance of apple blossoms. In summer, the grasses become a multicolored carpet of green with flecks of buttercup yellow, daisy white, and violet blue. Deep green leaves and pink-tinged blossoms appear like pieces of a giant jigsaw puzzle spread out haphazardly on a sky of blue cardboard. The drone of honey bees and the warmth of the sun ease the tensions that come from living the fast-paced life.

Christ had a habit of drawing aside from the noisy crowds that thronged Him to find a solitary place. "Whenever it was His privilege, He turned aside from the scene of His labor, to go into the fields, to meditate in the green valleys, to hold communion with God on the mountainside or amid the trees of the forest."[13] If He had not done this, He would have been powerless to face people every day, powerless to overcome temptations, powerless to live the sinless life.

Resolve to slow the pace. Stop entangling your life in a skein of duties, pleasures, and social obligations. The chaos of scrambled-maze life breaks backs and spirits. The growing, striving Christian must take time alone to fill up the loving cup again and again.

Jesus says, "Come to me, all you who are weary and burdened, and I will give you rest." Matthew 11:28, NIV. Here is a wonderful promise, but we must turn aside and seek His presence in order to receive that much-needed rest. The danger is that we will become tired or discouraged and cease to call on Him.[14] To neglect prayer or to pray only when it seems convenient will cause us to "lose . . . hold on God."[15] A convenient time will never come during the day if we wait. Our lives need the strength and peace only direct communion with God can bring. His peace can become our peace. Now is the time to find your own special place—a quiet sanctuary of the heart.

PATIENCE: Saints Under Stress

The strongest and noblest characters rest upon the foundation of patience and love, and trusting submission to the will of God.
—Ellen G. White

Christians are not immune or somehow miraculously shielded from all the ramifications of sin in this old world. Every corner of life is filled with pain, heartache, suffering, and cares that rob us of our patience and deplete our resources of love. There is the care and keeping of a home, the developing and disciplining of children, and relationships with spouse, workmates, and in-laws. Everyday living, work, play, education, health, and religion demand patience. Often those who try us and test us the most are the very ones who need our understanding the most.

A popular thought I've heard expressed is "Give me patience, Lord, and hurry." It speaks of a society that expects instant responses to all its demands, even for special virtues. We have been conditioned to expect immediate results for our wants and total satisfaction for all our needs. Hundreds of fast-food restaurants spew out tons of instant food; modern appliances give us clean clothes, hot meals, or frozen concoctions at the touch of a button; freeways bypass small towns and eliminate long waits at stoplights. We are geared to accelerated living. Is it any wonder parents abuse children when they feel unable to cope with stressful situations? How often does patience wear thin and do tempers flare in traffic jams? Is it surprising that children are unable to sit still at church? Patience is a lost virtue.

As impatience invades one corner of our lives, it quickly creeps into other areas. "It is not a great work and great battles alone which try the soul and demand courage. Everyday life brings its perplexities, trials, and discouragements. It is the humble work which frequently draws upon the patience and the fortitude."[1] Christians are not exempt from these problems. We are all vulnerable to the influence exerted on us by a variety of outside forces: society, parents, peers, work, children, spouse. At times, we all become victims of the instant-happiness trap, and patience quickly begins to shred and shrivel around the edges when things don't go exactly as planned.

One of the lesser-known stories of patience is found in the Old Testament. While Job is usually regarded as the man who had the greatest patience through suffering, we don't often think of any woman as his counterpart in biblical history. However, in the midst of war, violence, and famine there arises a woman of equal character whose example certainly qualifies her for a place in the Bible Hall of Fame. Her name was Rizpah, and she endured great sorrow, anguish, and hardship—probably more than any other woman in Scripture. She was a concubine in the court of Saul, Israel's first king. She lost her home, family, and wealth in one swift blow largely as a result of Saul's sins. She had lived in the luxurious fortress palace at Gibeah and was accustomed to the grand extravagances of the ruling class: beautiful clothes, obedient servants, fine food, elegant surroundings. Her bitter trial came suddenly, after Saul's suicide in battle, and it came about because of a promise he had broken.

Saul had endeavored to annihilate the Gibeonites despite a treaty Joshua had made with them. Some years after Saul died, they came to David (the new king) to seek redress for the broken agreement. They demanded that David hand over Saul's two sons by Rizpah, in addition to five of his grandsons. These seven innocent young men were taken out, slaughtered, and hanged on a hill near the palace. Rizpah, caught up in the center of this terrible revenge and murder, found herself alone and cast out into a desolate, barren land ravaged by war and drought. Grief-stricken, she took up her lonely watch near the bodies of her sons and stayed there for five months.[2]

We can only imagine the ghastly scene as Rizpah sat day after day in the scorching summer sun trying desperately to protect the rotting bodies. What a striking contrast between hatred and mother love. Days and weeks lengthened into months as she refused to abandon her beloved children. During the day she screamed at vultures and other birds of prey that would devour them. At night she dared not sleep for fear wild dogs would drag them away. After five months of vigilance, we picture a lone figure huddled in newly falling rain beside a pile of parched bones. See 2 Samuel 21:8-14.

The light of Rizpah's patience and loving sacrifice pierce a dark night in history. She represents all who have had to care for the terminally ill, the physically and mentally handicapped, the hurting, the sick, and the dying of every race since sin infected mankind. Every parent knows the anxious feeling that comes while sitting at the bedside of a sick, feverish child. Every one of us knows the feeling of standing beside the grave of a loved one. She gives hope and courage to millions who mourn or must bear tragedies of life patiently, quietly, and often alone.

One dictionary definition of patience is "calm and uncomplaining endurance, as under pain, provocation, etc."[3] It is the day-to-day circumstances of life that bring our greatest perplexities. But it is also these very things that bring our greatest sensitivities and refinement. There are as many situations as there are saints, and they all cry out for patience, endurance, and long-suffering. (I hesitate to use that last word, because it conjures up pictures of the "woe-is-me" type of martyr, long-suffering and insufferable. But you know the type of long-suffering I mean.)

One of the greatest problems in this area involves the seemingly endless times we spend waiting for other people. After all, don't we have more important things to do than wait in a doctor's office, an airline terminal, or a restaurant? What about the times spent waiting by the phone or looking for a stray sock or keeping supper warm until the whole family gets to the table? Children make us lose our patience when they are late coming home from school. Older folks stretch our patience often beyond the breaking point when they don't hear what we've said and we're forced to repeat ourselves again and again and.... Have any of us been lucky enough not to be delayed at a train crossing or stalled behind someone at a checkout counter? Ever notice how many of those tiny little wristwatch alarms go off at high noon in church? Impatience rears its ugly head even in the presence of God.

Let us think for a moment about God's patience with us. Where would we be without it? "Year after year He bears with our weakness and ignorance, with our ingratitude and waywardness. Notwithstanding all our wanderings, our hardness of heart, our neglect of His holy words, His hand is stretched out still."[4]

At the foot of the Matterhorn in Switzerland, side by side with the modern stations for the trams which swing gondola cars from valley floor to snowy peaks, stand ancient, stone-roofed huts. Inside these huts are small flocks of sheep wintering the Alpine storms. Fifteen or twenty rams, ewes, and lambs are protected in each of these tiny barns from the mountains' harsh weathers. At night, temperatures often plummet far below zero while snow accumulates on the roof and insulates the flock inside. Skiers by the thousands line up each day to catch the gondolas to the glaciers above the village of Zermatt. They trample past the wooden sheds without realizing there is life within them, unless the shepherd has come to tend his flock. Then the doors are thrown open as he cleans the stalls and spreads fresh straw.

On one particular afternoon I stopped to watch the activities of a shepherd and his tiny flock. While he was busy tending the ewes, a little lamb darted past him and out onto the icy path. The baby stood for a moment in the chill mountain air and looked in the direction of the noisy crowd nearby. Something startled him, and he ran. But he fell near a group of raucous skiers who laughed at his plight. Someone reached down to scoop him up, but he quickly gathered his legs under himself and ran bleating in another direction. A ewe inside the barn became frantic and tried to leap the railing. The rest of the flock caught her distress and jostled wildly. For several moments, all was chaos inside that tiny shed. Then, above the noise of the crowd and the bleating flock, I heard the shepherd call quietly to the lamb. There was no impatience, chastisement, or unhappiness in his voice, just calmness and understanding in his tone. The lamb stopped and turned to listen intently. Then he ran back to the safety of his home and master. The shepherd caught him up in his arms and held him gently.

So it is with us. An opportunity arises, a door opens, we see the outside world as freedom and fulfillment. We ignore the dangers and run out. Our loved ones frantically try to reach us. We don't listen to their cries or acknowledge their efforts to save us. But God knows where we are and understands our distress. All His wondrous love comes rushing back to us, and we hurry home. Remember *that* the next time you become discouraged or impatient with those who may be outside the fold and not in the safety of His arms. In the cold, in the dark, in the storm, in a hundred thousand ways, He sees, He cares, He never stops calling. They will hear. Be patient.

"We can rejoice, too, when we run into problems and trials for we know that they are good for us—they help us learn to be patient. And patience develops strength of character in us and helps us trust God more each time we use it until finally our hope and faith are strong and steady." Romans 5:3, 4, LB.

KINDNESS:
Welcome As the
Smiles of Angels

I expect to pass through this world but once. Any good therefore that I can do, or any kindness that I can show to any fellow creature, let me do it now. Let me not defer or neglect it, for I shall not pass this way again.

—Unknown author

The inspiration of that one thought has traveled around the world for more than a century. It has been attributed to several famous people, but no one seems to know its true origin. Christ expressed it another way when He said, "In everything, do to others what you would have them do to you, for this sums up the Law and the Prophets." Matthew 7:12, NIV. That simple, inspired verse is still the most important single rule of life, the basis of all moral and ethical principles on our planet.

Sacred history contains the names of many who were kind to others, gentle, and full of compassion. Pharaoh's daughter, who saved Moses from death and raised him as her son (see Exodus 2:5-10); John, the beloved disciple, who was so tenderhearted (see John 13:23); Dorcas, who gave so generously of her time and talents that her name became synonymous with acts of charity and good will (see Acts 9:36, 39); and Ruth, who gave up her homeland and family to care for her beloved mother-in-law (see Ruth 2:17, 18).

Gentleness makes a difference in lives. Kindness reaches hearts nothing else can touch. Kindness says, "I love you," "I care about you," "I want you to be my friend." We are told that there would be a hundred conversions to Christ where now there is only one if we would be kind and courteous.[1]

The title for this chapter came from *The Ministry of Healing*, page 158, "Words of kindness are as welcome as the smiles of angels." As I was searching for more information about kindness and how it could be applied to our daily lives, I found

41

these thumbnail thoughts in the *Index to the Writings of Ellen G. White* under "kindness": (1) We can relieve people's burdens and sorrows through acts of loving kindness. Perhaps that may mean digging deeper into our pockets, cupboards, or hearts. (2) When we instruct children, it should be with kindness. The soft touch, the encouraging word, the positive response. (3) Many people can be reached through kindness. Try doing something thoughtful without being found out. Don't expect congratulations or rewards for your efforts. Be a mysterious giver-of-gifts. Remain a secret pal. It is difficult to remain anonymous, because it is also delightful to be thanked for something we've done. The list goes on and on, and we are awed at the immense spectrum of influence one tiny word can have in our lives.

The phone company has a slogan, "Reach out and touch someone." It's a small, simple idea, but the potential is tremendous! One call can reach around the corner, across the country, or around the world. If you could see my phone bill, you would realize how frequently I have taken the phone company's advice! Sensitivity, awareness, and kindness can touch another heart that is aching or lonely. Is there someone somewhere who needs to hear the sound of your voice? Can your joy lift someone's heart today? Will your smile be remembered from springtime until long into the cold, lonely winter? Can you reach out and touch someone's life today with kindness?

When kindness is forgotten, we often strike out at the nearest thing—a door or the nearest wall, or perhaps a child or weaker adult. Abuse is the antithesis of kindness. And when kindness goes out the door, abuse has a way of sneaking in through the cracks. Anger can become a downward-spiraling whirlpool of destruction for us and those we love.

I mention this dark corner of our lives because the statistics on abuse in many hideous forms are becoming alarming. In 1978, every two minutes somewhere in the United States a child was being attacked, beaten, or abused by an adult.[2] Studies have shown that more than half of all abusive parents were themselves once victims of abuse. In many cases, if the abuse is allowed to continue, it can result in the crippling or death of the child. Christians are not immune to this disease.

It took me a long time to realize that many other people did not grow up in a loving, Christian home as I had. It had never occurred to me that the abuse problem might exist in the church family until I moved across the street from such a situation several years ago. Time has since cured the problem, but it was not unusual in those days to hear angry voices coming from a particular house. At times it was frightening. Tension ran high in the neighborhood when it happened, and everyone bristled with awareness. We often worried about the child's safety, but she never appeared to be physically abused, so we said nothing. The child's only defense was her ability to outrun her mother. The screen door would fly open, then slam shut as the little girl would run to hide somewhere in the neighborhood until her mother cooled down. At church on Sabbath mornings they would both appear perfectly normal. On Sunday afternoons the screen door would burst open yet again as the whole scene would be repeated.

Have you ever yelled at your children in a less-than-kind manner? I have. Show me a parent who hasn't, and I'll show you a perfect parent. (There is no such person.) I have had to apologize several times to my two because frustrations got the better of me and brought out the worst in me. I said some pretty unkind things and regretted it deeply—usually the split second after I yelled.

It is difficult, if not impossible, to assess the damage done to a child by verbal abuse. We can only wonder at the irreparable psychological harm done by a lifestyle in which the environment is constantly hostile and threatening. Physical injuries often heal and disappear, but emotional scars may remain for a lifetime. Psychiatric wards, mental hospitals, and prisons are filled with the victims.

Whether the abuse springs from a stressful job that is hated, a marriage that has turned sour, problem children, an insufferable invalid in the home, the loss of a loved one, or "just a general feeling that you're too precious for life to treat you this way, there is but one answer. Look at Jesus Christ. As He is."[3] When we look at Him, we discover kindness that comes from a Spirit-filled life. A passive virtue, kindness is an essential grace.[4]

The Christian life should be taken more seriously than it is. In addition to gentleness and kindness, "there is need of courage, force, energy, and perseverance."[5] With these positive forces come enthusiasm and zeal to complete a work begun centuries ago. "Jesus, the precious Saviour, the pattern man, was firm as a rock where truth and duty were concerned. And His life was a perfect illustration of true courtesy. Kindness and gentleness gave fragrance to His character. He had ever a kind look and a word of comfort and consolation for the needy and oppressed."[6]

"Thou hast also given me the shield of thy salvation: and thy gentleness hath made me great." 2 Samuel 22:36.

GOODNESS: Creative Living

This is a cause worth living for—Wherever we go we find opportunities of doing good.—Narcissa Whitman

I looked at the parched ground and dried bunch grass and wondered whether it was better to die on a beautiful day among friends or on a dismal day when even the weather was an enemy. I turned and looked beyond the vast, waving inland sea of prairie grass to the Blue Mountains the Whitmans crossed on their trek to this wilderness. Shimmering heat waves played over the valley, and beyond it as far as the eye could see stretched plains and mountains. A few yards from where I stood, a range of small hills rose to meet the bright summer sky. In springtime the meadows are speckled with wild flowers, and in the winter they are buried beneath snow and ice. The birds sang sweetly, and the crickets buzzed in the heat. This view I see now, I thought, was the last thing their eyes ever saw.

In 1847, Marcus and Narcissa Whitman and twelve others were massacred at the mission station just a few miles from where Walla Walla College now stands. They became martyrs in a lonely land at the hands of strangers they had come to help. In 1836, Narcissa and another young white woman by the name of Eliza Spalding were the first women to cross the Rocky Mountains to enter the western frontier. They had come with their husbands from New York state to help establish Christian missions in the remote wilderness of Oregon, Washington, and Idaho, known then as the Oregon Territory.

Today, only a dry river bed remains where the waters rushed by the Whitman home, the waters which so cruelly claimed the

45

life of their only child, Alice, in 1839. The hills mentioned in diaries are still there, however, and one of them thrusts a monument into the azure sky in their honor. Marcus built a bench for Narcissa on top of this hill, and she went there often to view the valley. To the east is an inspiring view of the Blue Mountain range, and far to the west in the direction of old Fort Walla Walla the hills stand like silent sentinels.[1]

The Whitmans' story is one of goodness, dedication, and sacrifice. It is also the story of the beginnings of missionary contacts in the West. In one of her journals, Narcissa described the trip across the vast frontier as "an unheard of journey for females."[2] She rode horseback sidesaddle for much of the way, because the wagons had a nasty habit of tipping over. A short time after reaching Fort Walla Walla, her friend, Eliza, left to establish another mission station over a hundred miles away. The isolation and loneliness of the prairie wilderness settled in on the two women. They agreed to keep in touch by thought, and at 9:00 every morning they isolated themselves for a brief period to think and pray for each other. Alone-together they drew on inner strengths which gave them hope to carry on. Narcissa wrote, "The Lord *has provided & 'the Lord will provide' for us,* even to the *end of our pilgrimage here.*"[3]

Today, the mass grave and monument are all that marks the spot where these brave pioneers fell in the rain and mud. The house, which was made of split logs fitted into grooved posts, with a roof of poles covered with straw and mud, has long since been claimed by earth, time, and archaeologists. Hardship, loneliness, disease, poverty, and death thousands of miles from civilization were the order of the day, but so long as they lived they labored on. What joy will be theirs when they awake to find that their labors were not lost in the prairie winds. "Then shall the King say unto them on his right hand, Come, ye blessed of my Father, inherit the kingdom prepared for you from the foundation of the world." Matthew 25:34.

Modern technology has shrunk our planet to a global village in which radio and television and communications satellites bring canned religion into our living rooms with the push of a button. Jet planes fly out of the airport at Walla Walla, Washington, every day to a thousand places the early pioneers never dreamed of. The Oregon Trail has been paved over by superhighways all the way from Independence, Missouri, to Astoria on the Oregon coast. Only ruts remain in some isolated, untraveled areas where weather and time work in tandem to erode their memory. As more and more people are reached by mass communication and transportation systems, there is less and less need for the gospel to be told one-to-one.

But there is one thing that has not changed—loneliness. Progress has not brought us any closer together than Narcissa and Eliza were in 1840. In many ways, we are perhaps more lonely on our own little prairies of modern isolation. Most of us live in single-family dwellings, compartmentalized high-rises, or isolated condominium cubicles. Mechanical gadgets tell us we can dispense with the need for sympathetic, caring friends. We often think more about the success of an artificial heart than we do about the human ones. People are uncommunicative in crowded cities and isolated in country areas. Indeed, many church congregations ignore the visitor or the stranger who shows up uninvited or unaccompanied on Sabbath morning.

Physical survival is maintained largely by dialing toll-free numbers. But you can't dial the corner supermarket and order a dozen friends. You can't call your family physician and request a prescription to pick up a friend or two at the local pharmacy. Friendships still can't be bought. Real friends, true friends, intimate friends don't come in cellophane-wrapped packages ready to use when needed. They come maybe two or three to a lifetime, if you're lucky. They are scarce, very precious, and definitely priceless.

Like the warm bond created by the first settlers in the West, it is a deep, personal relationship with another human being that allows us to see inwardly more clearly. Like looking into a mirror ringed with bright lights, the beauties as well as the imperfections are discernible. And although the reflection may not be to our liking, it is necessary and valuable if we are to be honest with ourselves. "That's the true test of friendship, Lord. Not when we feel luckier and stronger, when we can reach *down* to help somebody. But when we feel less lucky, our importance threatened; when we've got to reach *up* to give."[4] Goodness can only be shared by touching, caring, and loving others very deeply.

Her name was Dorcas, and she had dozens of friends. She loved people, and her claim to fame rested on the fact that she was "full of good works." Acts 9:36. When she died, she was so sincerely missed that God through Peter resurrected her. She was beloved in her hometown of Joppa. She was a profound example of goodness, dedication to duty, and the value of having friends. Her name has become synonymous with doing good for the benefit of others. "Her qualification for a place in God's gallery of victors was not her skill as a theologian or her fortitude as a martyr, but her diligence as a seamstress. The fruits of her salvation were revealed in her skillful handling of a needle."[5] She took some thread and embroidered her name across the pages of sacred history. Whether she was well-off by the standards of her day or living in poverty in Joppa's shantytown we are not told; besides, it makes no difference. The point is, she saw a need and filled it to the best of her ability. The size of her pocketbook had nothing to do with the size of her heart. Charitable acts are not restricted to the wealthy. Service to the needy, destitute, and hungry is not limited to the affluent. Dorcas obviously took whatever she had, large or small, and stitched God's love into every part of it. He multiplied her revenue and blessed her endeavors, and His love and goodness flowed through her into the lives of others. See Acts 9:36-42.

There is goodness, kindness, and a portion of Dorcas in all of us. But we fear giving more of ourselves, because we worry about imaginary hazards that may be waiting around the corner or in the shadows. We hold back spontaneous giving because we are fearful of not having enough left over for ourselves. We purposely avoid becoming involved, because we think it may require more time, money, or effort than we are willing to expend. It is less threatening to think about starving people on other continents thousands of miles from our kitchen table than to help the destitute at some soup kitchen in town.

The other problem with goodness is that it appears to be so

dull. Yet goodness brings happiness, and the most exciting thing in the world is happiness. The miracle of universal happiness has eluded us for ages and seems to remain unattainable. Values have been turned upside down, and doing good appears to be unexciting and unrewarding. Sensationalism and violence attract so much more attention. That is why terrorism makes headlines while charity is hidden on an inside page.

Several months ago, stuck away in a corner of an issue of the local conference newsletter, was a story about another couple from Walla Walla. A member of the Dorcas Society in her local church, the woman had sewed 229 quilt tops in a year. She was 87 years old. Her husband, who was 91, had helped her.[6] Charitable deeds are not limited to the young or the rich or the highly skilled among us. Like Dorcas and Narcissa Whitman, this Christian couple are helping others and stitching God's love into their work. The goodness of the pioneers and of the first missionaries lives on in Walla Walla's valley.

In England in 1800, Elizabeth Fry married a banker and settled down to enjoy the comfortable life. In the next fifteen years, she had ten children. That fact alone could have prevented her from serving outside her home, but it was just the beginning of a life filled with selfless caring for others. In 1813, at the urging of a visiting American Quaker, she visited Newgate prison in London, and her life was never the same again.

Elizabeth must have shuddered when the jailers bolted the doors behind her. Such a stench filled her nostrils that she must have gagged as she was led down dark, dank corridors. Surely she grasped her elegant skirts around her with one hand and steadied herself with the other to keep from slipping in the filth. Like caged animals, the women and children clawed and screamed at her through iron bars. Dirty, sick babies clung to their mothers, and some of the very young sat huddled in corners weeping because they were deserted. Elizabeth stayed only as long as her senses could endure; and after she climbed back out of this living tomb into the cold, fresh air of England, her feelings of disgust for the appalling conditions burned in her mind for the rest of her life.

Since the Middle Ages, when prisons began replacing the

dungeons of ancient times, thousands of women and children just like these were incarcerated together in overcrowded, unsanitary, vermin-infested cells for crimes ranging from petty theft to murder. Three years following her first visit, Elizabeth returned to help the miserable captives. She arranged for school rooms to be set up to prepare the women and children for release back into society. In 1818, in defense of her prison school, she became the first woman to appear before the House of Commons Committee on Prisons. She continued to do what she could to alleviate the suffering of those behind bars, and in her spare time she began taking medical supplies and food to prisoners on board ships destined for the penal colonies. In twenty-five years she visited over one hundred ships and approximately 12,000 convicts.

In the winter of 1820, she provided shelter for homeless street people. By 1821, she started visiting prisons in northern England and Scotland. She became interested in improving the treatment of the mentally ill in the British hospital system. In 1840, she founded a home to train nurses. Between 1838 and 1843, she visited prisons in France, Switzerland, Germany, Belgium, Holland, and Denmark. She died in 1845 at the age of 65, having completed an unselfish life dedicated to doing good for others.[7]

Along our pathway are many people who are caged by destructive habits, wearying jobs, and frustrating lifestyles. We can help to set them free. The young are apprehensive and anxious about the future; the middle-aged suffer the pressures of competition and stress in professional pursuits; older folks face their retirement—in many cases—with limited incomes, poor health, and alienation of family and friends. These people feel lonely, helpless, and discouraged. Many are trapped by circumstances over which they have no control.

There are a million ways we can help to set them free and lift their spirits to soar again. Try mentioning some of their admirable qualities. Send a postcard or small gift of appreciation. Make a phone call, brief and to the point. Send flowers or money when appropriate. Take them to lunch. Tell them you love them. It will change *your* life.

The first time the gates of Newgate prison slammed shut behind Elizabeth Fry, she surely must have wondered why she had come. After all, what could one person do? It's not that she didn't have aspirations or the urge to help—we all have those feelings—but invariably, the nagging thought must have troubled her as it must have crossed Narcissa's mind, "I am just one person." How often have you heard someone say, "One person probably won't make any difference"? After all, what can any one of us do that could possibly make an ounce of difference in this doomed world? If this is our attitude, we are doomed. We may as well quit, because nothing is going to happen where that type of attitude prevails. One writer has said, "If we would walk with God, let us put on our seven league boots and be unafraid."[8] Now, I've never seen a pair of seven-league boots; I doubt they even exist. But I imagine they would be worthy of any task set before them. I tried on Father's wading boots once, the boots he used for middle-of-the-river fishing. I found I could splash through mud puddles up to my hips without getting wet. Even blackberry patches were no obstacle when I was protected by those sturdy boots. The Christian is counseled to put on the whole armor of Christ. With such protection, we are invincible. See Ephesians 6:13.

We are tempted to say that the heroes of the past were exceptional people, somehow more gifted or talented than we. History cuts across such disparaging remarks with the records of lives like Florence Nightingale, whose strict rules of cleanliness were her prescription for the wounded of the Crimean War; Clara Barton, whose singular work led to the establishment of the Red Cross; and Abraham Lincoln, who was inspired to great leadership by a mother who cared. When he was asked to name the greatest book he ever read, Lincoln answered, "My mother." Were these people exceptional? Their own words convince us that this was not the case. "I had faith: that was all," said Florence Nightingale.[9] Without exception, the great works of the world began with one person. The great religions, the masterful inventions, the lofty empires were all built on the initiative and enthusiasm of solitary minds. How then can any of us say, "I am just one person"?

The psalmist tells us, "Surely goodness and love will follow me all the days of my life, and I will dwell in the house of the Lord forever." Psalm 23:6, NIV. This bold statement implies complete confidence and trust in a Saviour who controls lives and destinies. How often do we feel that no matter what occurs in our lives, we are being led by His great love and goodness? It is easy to be happy when life is sunshine and lollipops. But what about the helpless times of illness? When my world, my relationships, my home, or my body is falling apart at the seams, what then? Do pious platitudes crumble along with sand-castle dreams and hopes? In the midst of grief and pain, can I say with confidence, "In all things God works for the good of those who love him"? Romans 8:28, NIV.

Each day is filled with new opportunities and challenges. The promise of Psalm 23 is God's assurance that an inexhaustible supply of goodness comes from a heart filled with love and compassion. Whether we are ministering to strangers in a foreign land, easing the suffering of captives behind metal bars or mental barriers, or quietly shaping and molding hearts around the home fires, God's promises follow us, and " 'The Lord will provide' for us, even to the *end of our pilgrimage here.*"

"With this in mind, we constantly pray for you, that our God may count you worthy of his calling, and that by his power he may fulfill every good purpose of yours and every act prompted by your faith." 2 Thessalonians 1:11, NIV.

FAITHFULNESS: Miry Pits and Spiritual Radar

And thus we, night-wanderers through a stormy and dismal world, if we bear the lamp of Faith, enkindled at a celestial fire, it will surely lead us home to that heaven whence its radiance was borrowed.—Nathaniel Hawthorne

The trees in the park looked like dead roots turned upside down against the steel-gray dawn. A giant clock, created from living plants, silently marked the time, even though the flowers were frozen around its circumference. It was midwinter in Europe, and the city of Geneva, Switzerland, slept.

I walked in silence across the bridge, Pont du Mont Blanc, and except for a few seagulls crouched on the piling, the city seemed devoid of life. Lace curtains were still drawn against the chill of the outside world. Narrow cobblestone streets named Rue du Prince and Rue de la Fontaine pointed the way to the cathedral on the hill. I pulled my coat closer and began the long climb.

The church was an imposing structure with a single spire and two concrete towers which rose over the city like a giant fortress. I stood at its base, suddenly dwarfed by its massiveness. Awe pressed in on me. I was walking on stones which knew the feet of saints and martyrs over 400 years ago. I felt for a moment that I should remove my shoes, for this was holy ground. The crucible of the sixteenth century, the cradle of the Protestant Reformation, the beginning of enlighted religious doctrines. The streets here are named for men of the stature of John Calvin and William Farel. In the nearby park, Promenade des Bastions, Calvin, Farel, Bèze, and Knox stand side by side in larger-than-life statues. I stood for a long time gazing at these courageous men and thanked God silently for them.

From deep within the cathedral's heart I could hear organ

music—an early-morning practice session. But I was too early for services. Who would stand behind the pulpit John Calvin once occupied? What would be the subject of the sermon that morning? I shall never know, because time did not permit me to linger. There were people to meet, schedules to keep, and a day just beginning. I had to be content to stand there and absorb the sights and feel in my heart the omnipresent power of the Reformation message. It is alive four centuries later. It echoes through the corridors of the old cathedral, it resounds off the cobblestones of the surrounding streets, it cries from the statues in the park, "Salvation and righteousness come by faith!" In the midst of a spiritual darkness blacker than night, the great Reformers kindled fires whose flames have glowed with the brightness of noonday for hundreds of years.

When we are bogged down in troubles, when we are groping for answers, when we can't see beyond tomorrow or even to the end of today, faith reaches out in the darkness and grasps the hand of God. In modern-day terms, Corrie ten Boom said, "Faith is like radar which sees through the fog—the reality of things at a distance that the human eye cannot see."[1] Faith to the Reformers was the faith of Hebrews 11:1, NIV, "Now faith is being sure of what we hope for and certain of what we do not see." And it was the faith of Ephesians 2:8, "By grace are ye saved through faith; and that not of yourselves: it is the gift of God."

A month following her high-school graduation, Joni Eareckson broke her neck in a tragic diving accident and was permanently paralyzed from the shoulders down. Out of her despair, she turned to God and found faith and guidance in her life. "When I start to brood and complain and grumble about my situation, what helps me is to get a higher view of God—to lift my eyes up out of the miry pits and look at how great He is."[2] She went on to become a writer, counselor, painter, singer, and lecturer. Without such determination and faith, she might have wallowed about in the bogs of self-pity as an emotionally helpless cripple. Her faith was not simply a feeling or a fantasy, but a higher awareness of her Saviour. She sought Him and found Him to be greater than she had ever imagined.

King David, whose life was a constant struggle from bottomless pits to spectacular peaks, said, "I waited patiently for the Lord; and he inclined unto me, and heard my cry. He brought me up also out of an horrible pit, out of the miry clay, and set my feet upon a rock, and established my goings." Psalm 40:1, 2.

Sometimes it takes a traumatic experience to build faith into our lives. At times God allows us to be knocked down in the mainstream of life so that dramatic changes can take place. It is often only the swift, unexpected blow that brings us to our knees at the foot of the Cross. From this position the only direction to look is upward, and by faith we are drawn nearer to our Saviour.

As part of love's kaleidoscope, faith spreads patterns of exquisite color and harmony through our lives. Faith means counting on God when we don't know what tomorrow holds. "There is nothing that so fully clinches faith as to be so sure of the answer [to prayer] that you can thank God for it."[3] When things fall apart at the seams, faith keeps us from indulging in varying degrees of self-pity, guilt, and remorse. Faith reassures us that nothing about God ever changes, only our lives change. "Faith . . . takes hold of Omnipotence and refuses to be baffled."[4] It is possible to care for the sick and suffering all day, and then, when they die the next, feel that you are defeated and your faith has failed you. It is possible to present ten Bible studies a week and then feel discouraged when your students make their own decisions to follow another course. It is possible to be a missionary with a burning desire to heal and help, and still become depressed when things don't go just the way you planned them.

I found a story recently in a diary from the 1860s. While their parents were away for the evening, two young children and a baby were left alone in a large farmhouse. One of them set the baby on a table. The infant promptly kicked the kerosene lamp onto the floor. Flames shot up. The young girl, who had been taught to pray, suggested they try that approach. The older brother, perceiving the situation as the potential disaster it could become, told her to wait a minute while he threw the lamp outside.[5]

While some stand idly by, wringing their hands in despair, God has others who seize the problem with both hands and save the day. "The only thing that counts is faith expressing itself through love." Galatians 5:6, NIV. Faith alone would not have quenched the kerosene fire. Faith alone would not have wrought the Protestant Reformation. Faith alone would not have brought the Adventist Church to where it is today. Pioneer faith put works into action, and faith and works achieved results. To assume that God will take care of everything without my help is a sin—the sin of presumption. To believe that all is lost and nothing I do will matter is another sin— the sin of despair. Presumption and despair are the antithesis of faith.

Hebrews 11 is called the Bible's faith chapter. It is filled with faith and action. It is not filled with plaster saints like those in Europe's great cathedrals. It is filled with sinners who overcame by faith. It is loaded with adventure, endurance, and encouragement written "between the lines." It is full of down-to-earth, practical examples of Christian faith in action. It is not a fanciful fairytale, but focuses on realism. By faith, Abraham looked for a heavenly city (see verse 10); by faith, Jochebed saved Moses from Pharaoh's death decree (see verse 23); by faith, Rahab was saved when the walls of Jericho fell (see verse 31). "Faith is trusting God—believing that He loves us and knows best what is for our good. Thus, instead of our own, it leads us to choose His way."[6]

We find later on in Scripture that patience, endurance, obedience, and faithfulness are the necessary characteristics of God's remnant people. "This calls for patient endurance on the part of the saints who obey God's commandments and remain faithful to Jesus." Revelation 14:12, NIV. We are not on a playground. The world is a battlefield, an arena to the entire universe. The last hours of earth's history will require a faith that will endure to the end.

Moses is, perhaps, one of the most excellent examples of living faith. From bulrushes to palace, from desert to mountaintop, from poverty on earth to riches in heaven—what a life he led! Through joy and sorrow, water and fire, war and peace! But without his mother's faith, he would have become nothing but mud along the banks of the Nile.

Washington Irving once wrote, "There is in every true woman's heart a spark of heavenly fire, which lies dormant in the broad daylight of prosperity; but which kindles up, and beams and blazes in the dark hour of adversity."[7] Jochebed had that spark of heavenly fire. I believe that spark was faith.

If there were an eleventh commandment, I think it would be "Thou shalt not fall prey to the Chicken-Little syndrome." You remember Chicken Little, the poor bird that got clobbered by an acorn and immediately thought the sky was falling. The clouds may hang low, the storms may rage, but the sky won't fall. Faith and hope need to reach out even in the darkest night and seek the light. Doom and gloom have no place in the Christian life, yet many of us fall victim to this insipid disease. We let tiny, worrisome acorns of doubt convince us that all is lost, and we run around like the chicken, broadcasting our concern to everyone who cares to listen. Instead of praying, "God, I believe; help thou mine unbelief," we loudly proclaim, "I have my doubts." And like poor Chicken Little we begin to believe them.

One of the most descriptive statements about faith can be found in a little book called *Can God Be Trusted?* Read the entire book for yourself, but Graham Maxwell has this to say about faith: "Faith, as I understand it, is a word we use to describe a relationship with God as with a person well known. The better we know Him, the better this relationship may be.

"Faith implies an attitude toward God of love, trust, and deepest admiration. It means having enough confidence in Him, based on the more than adequate evidence revealed, to be willing to believe whatever He says, to accept whatever He offers, and to do whatever He wishes—without reservation—for the rest of eternity."[8]

Faith is not shown by snake handling, poison drinking, or other foolish acts to prove that God will miraculously spare our lives. Faith is a day-to-day experience, a growing grace, an honored virtue. It is a gift from God through His Holy Spirit. It is another aspect of love's kaleidoscope. Sunlight consists of various colors blended into brilliance. So faith, which is a gift of the Spirit, helps to constitute love in all its beauty. It gives us wings to rise above the problem, the frustration, the grief of a tragedy in our lives. It lifts us up when we would fall in the mud. It makes us whistle in the darkness or sing in the rain. It takes us to His presence, because as we reach up, He reaches more than half way down to lift us higher.

"Let us hold fast the profession of our faith without wavering; (for he is faithful that promised;) and let us consider one another to provoke unto love and to good works." Hebrews 10:23, 24.

GENTLENESS: Dear Hearts and Gentle People

True gentleness is a gem of great value in the sight of God.
—Ellen G. White

Somewhere between the stoic who is strongwilled and represses all emotions and the chronic complainer who whimpers over every tiny problem is the Christian who is aware of his abilities and shortcomings and chooses to let Christ control every aspect of his life. When life's little annoyances or great catastrophes occur, this person does not let them overflow into depression, remorse, or guilt. Somewhere between the saint whose prayer life is a constant vigil and the sinner who senses no need of spiritual support is the person who is consciously aware of God's presence and chooses to be lead in the gentle pathway of His love.

At times we have all been plagued with negative thoughts. "I am tired and growing older faster than I care to admit." (We all are.) "I am bored and lonely most of the time, even to the point of depression and despair." (God never promised rainbows without rain.) You may even feel that you are useless to anyone, especially God. (It's simply not true.) You may know you are a burden on someone. How can you be gentle under these circumstances? You may feel you are no longer in love or loved by anyone. There are endless nights without sleep. It is difficult, if not impossible, to be gentle when the frustration level in your life is at an all-time high. But it is at this point of utter desperation when you should see that you cannot handle your problems alone. No one can. Whether your problems have been plaguing you for years or for only a matter of hours, you should realize that you can't solve all your problems by yourself. May I suggest that God can.

Don't be unhappy because you aren't doing what you want to do, or you aren't where you want to be, or you aren't making progress as quickly as you had hoped. God can handle that. He said, "In the world ye shall have tribulation: but be of good cheer; I have overcome the world." John 16:33. Don't attempt to take on the whole world by yourself. It can't be done. The place to find gentleness to overcome these obstacles is in Jesus.

Someone has described gentleness as a placid, unaffected grandfather clock that goes on at its own pace during a thunderstorm. This does not mean that you should remain totally oblivious to a disaster happening at your feet. It means that an external catastrophe will not leave you a physical or emotional wreck, that in spite of frustrations, you will go on because of a gentle spirit within that cannot be disrupted from without. We see this quality in the nurse tending the critically ill or the teacher carefully instructing his pupils. We find it in the mother and father who patiently, gently wait for their children to learn the important values in life by example and experience. They make the best of their lives where they are, and they do their finest work regardless of circumstances. They do it without regret or self-pity.

A Christian must build and grow where he is. There is a solemn pride which comes from knowing that you are doing your best wherever God has called you to serve. You may be chief of staff at the local hospital or chief-cook-and-bottle-washer at home. You may be top executive secretary or last man on the carpool list. You may be a part-time laborer or a full-time Mom. The point is, no matter where, no matter what, no matter who you are, you are always top priority with God. You come first with Him. Does He come first with you? "The relations between God and each soul are as distinct and full as though there were not another soul upon the earth to share His watchcare, not another soul for whom He gave His beloved Son."[1] You are always at the top of God's list. It matters to Him about you. Nothing you do is ever unimportant to Him. Nothing happens to you that is ever ignored by Him. Knowing that, how can you ever say again that you are lonely, bored, or unloved?

Christ was the epitome of gentleness. He risked Himself and dared to change the world. He did it with love and gentleness. He didn't beat anyone into submission on His way to achieving that goal. The only stick He ever carried was the one they nailed Him to.

Gentleness is not weakness. Meekness is not lack of strength. Strength does not come from a stick or a clenched fist or a loud voice screaming commands. God needs your gentle spirit to care for others, to share as He shared, to love people into His kingdom. He needs the dear, gentle hearts of His people to show His love for all mankind.

Christ said, "Blessed are the meek: for they shall inherit the earth." Matthew 5:5.

SELF-CONTROL: Trailblazers and Goal Setters

God is preparing His heroes; and when opportunity comes, He can fit them into their place in a moment, and the world will wonder where they came from.—A. B. Simpson

The life of the Seventh-day Adventist Christian is not soaring from one silver-lined cloud to another. Neither is it dwelling in some dark, dismal cave. Henry Thoreau said, "Birds do not sing in caves."[1] God doesn't need emotionally crippled cave-dwellers. What He does need are people with a sense of direction, singleness of purpose, and willing hearts.

"Where there is no vision, the people perish." Proverbs 29:18. It seems that very few people today have a vision, a goal, a direction in which they are traveling. Very few seem to know where they are heading, let alone how they plan to get there. Many never set goals, and others allow themselves to be distracted along the way. Many have received acclaim when they have risen to great heights of personal achievement only to languish thereafter for lack of additional goals and plans.

Self-control, or self-discipline, requires deciding about priorities in one's life. Priorities naturally lead to goal-setting, and setting goals should be at the top of every Christian's priority list. To set a goal means to take affirmative action by charting a destination and direction for yourself. For that is what a goal really is—a place you want to go.

At one time or another, most of us have been aware of our faults and bad habits and have tried to correct them. We strive for personal improvement and seek to make the most of our abilities. But self-discipline is not easy. The greatest test of character is how one takes charge of his own life.

No modern romance novel will ever exceed the beauty and

simplicity of the love story of Isaac and Rebekah recorded for us in the twenty-fourth chapter of Genesis. This ancient biblical narrative with its idyllic, fascinating sequence of events, captures our curiosity and leaves an indelible imprint on our hearts. It is one of the chapters in the chain of God-directed events leading to the first advent of Christ.

Rebekah, the beautiful young heroine, became part of that eternal chain. She was barely twenty years old when she left home and family to become the bride of a stranger in a distant land. She was a goal setter, an ancient trailblazer. When asked if she would go with Abraham's servant, she replied that she would, which showed obvious courage and conviction. Believing that God had selected her to be Isaac's bride, she gathered together her possessions and set out on a great caravan journey to a place she had never seen before. They "crossed the banks of the Euphrates into the pathless and sun-bleached sands of the desert . . . over the Lebanon highlands into the green hills of Galilee and finally drew near the yellow plains around Beer-sheba."[2]

Isaac had gone for a walk at sundown when he saw the party approaching. The Bible says when Rebekah saw him, she covered her face with a veil. It must have been love at first sight, because without going into lengthy details the Bible recorder tells us, "Isaac brought her into the tent of his mother Sarah, and he married Rebekah. So she became his wife, and he loved her." Genesis 24:67, NIV. Rebekah remained Isaac's true love as long as she lived.

From Abraham, the lineage traveled down through Isaac and Rebekah to Jacob, to Boaz and Ruth, to Jesse, the father of David, then on down through the centuries to "Joseph, the husband of Mary, of whom was born Jesus, who is called Christ." Matthew 1:16, NIV. What beautiful parts they all played in this eternal story.

Direction in life has very little to do with how fast or how far one travels at any given period in time. But it has a great deal to do with where we place our footsteps every day. Christian growth is gradual and not always perceptible overnight. Progress in character-building takes more than a minute, an hour, or a day. It is the work of a lifetime.[3] Character is not fixed, but grows and unfolds from day to day. When we allow the kaleidoscope of love into our lives through the Holy Spirit we are able to form characters after His image. "Not because of our lovely characters, but because of His."[4]

One of the greatest mistakes we can make is to start believing our own feelings and experiences. When we base our decisions exclusively on inner thoughts and moods, hunches, or speculation, we become like existentialists who believe that life and the great universe are without real direction or purpose. Every problem in life that you will ever confront is recorded somewhere in God's Word. If you can't find the section that speaks to your particular problem or condition, ask a wiser Christian. But first accept the challenge to hunt for an answer as if you were digging in some vast archaeological field. You will discover other hidden treasures nearby that may become the answer to other problems.

We wouldn't think of beginning a long journey to a place we had never been without checking a map. "There isn't a human mind brilliant enough, nor a human heart spiritually enlightened enough to be able to see God's entire plan."[5] He alone can see the future, and by faith we reach out and take hold of His hand because we know He will lead us to our ultimate goal—heaven.

Samuel Rutherford said, "Believe God's word and power more than you believe your own feelings and experiences. Your Rock is Christ, and it is not the Rock which ebbs and flows, but your sea."[6] We all learn by our experiences and mistakes, but we must not lean on them as crutches. We must build with God's direction, because we are free to do so. We must pick up the pieces and choose how we shall use them to shape, mold, and build our future. Our destiny has very little to do with financial status, social standing in the community, rank of office in the church, or exceptional talent. It is determined by the attitude which prevails in our lives. It depends where our predominant thoughts are centered. It matters what has won mastery of our hearts. "Discipline of mind and body is one of the most difficult things one has to acquire, but in the long run it is a valuable ingredient of education and a tremendous bulwark in time of trouble."[7]

Those who merely cope, drifting along from one day to another with no sense of direction, with no better plan than just living for the moment, are leaving all to chance and unforeseen fortune. In one famous children's story, the heroine says:

> "Would you tell me, please, which way I
> ought to go from here?"
> "That depends a good deal on where you want
> to get to," said the Cat.
> "I don't much care where—" said Alice.
> "Then it doesn't matter which way you go," said the Cat.[8]

Those who don't plan ahead are "floaters" like Alice in Wonderland; their lives drift like feathery, wind-blown dandelion seeds on currents of insecurity. Self-control and goal setting are inseparable in the Christian life. In Hebrews, we are admonished to "throw off everything that hinders and the sin that so easily entangles, and let us run with perseverance the race marked out for us." Hebrews 12:1, NIV.

I live in a city where maintaining physical fitness has become a lifestyle for many. People are running, biking, swimming, jogging, and participating in all types of exercise programs to get into better physical shape. Most of these people have two things in common: They are goal setters, and they are highly disciplined. They must lay off excess baggage (weight) before they can compete. They must not procrastinate, because to do so would mean falling back into old habits. They must be patient, because training takes time and effort. And if they quit, even in the last quarter mile of a race, they will have lost.

Someone has attempted to outline the Christian race in this manner, dividing the experience into three main phases:

1. The first part seems relatively easy, and we are inclined to say that it doesn't take much effort to be a Christian. "Live one day at a time and don't sin!" Sounds simple. I haven't sinned for the last half hour. "This is easy."

2. Then one day things don't go as we'd planned. The bottom falls out, and we're going under for the third time. The realization begins to dawn, "This is hard."

3. Time passes. Storm clouds of doubt and depression hang around our house. Anger and frustration become permanent guests who refuse to leave, and we cry out, "This is impossible."

From a human standpoint, it is impossible—we can't do it. Excess baggage (the old, sinful habits) weighs us down. Unbelief says, "God can't carry me over the rough spots." An indifferent attitude tells us that it doesn't matter whether we run well or not, just so long as we make it over the finish line. Procrastination never gets us off the starting line. Depression makes us quit. Hardship makes us change the course to something more comfortable and compromising. Panic says, "I'm not going to make it." Pride—in spite of the evidence—boasts, "I can handle it." If we could handle it, we'd all be gods. There is only One who can part the waters and calm the storm. All of the above excuses short-circuit God's efforts to build our characters along the route to heaven.

Turning your eyes on Jesus requires turning your back on sin, disbelief, the negative attitude, procrastination, depression, hardship, panic, and pride. "Let us fix our eyes on Jesus, the author and perfecter of our faith." Hebrews 12:2, NIV. By directing our thoughts and pathways toward higher goals, we are drawn closer to Christ.

Goals require making life-altering decisions and blazing trails where others may not have ventured before. Robert Frost wrote:

> I shall be telling this with a sigh
> Somewhere ages and ages hence:
> Two roads diverged in a wood, and I—
> I took the one less traveled by,
> And that has made all the difference. [9]

The Seventh-day Adventist Christian certainly chooses the road "less traveled by," and that choice most definitely makes a great deal of difference every step of the way.

All too many of the support groups, crisis centers, and social programs of today seem to focus on one basic approach—eliminating the negatives and clutter from lives. They zero in on removing whatever it is that ails a person. In some cases, they seek to remove possessions as well, Rather than providing nourishment which would enrich basic existence, incredible amounts of energy are expanded in finding a place to dump life's garbage. The result is that a vast vacuum remains when no further plans are made to fill life with positive attitudes and goals.

It is true that we can unclutter ourselves of belongings and things, time-consuming committees, endless meetings, regrets about what we did or did not do, anxieties, bad habits, and meaningless relationships. But we are only "cardboard"* Christians until we fill those vacancies to overflowing with the attributes of Christ which give real meaning to life and after-life.

The successful Christian manages the normal, predictable crises and learns to master the greater calamities such as accidents, death, and financial setbacks. The Christian personality should be characterized by an outgoing, eternally optimistic nature, not by a ridiculous fantasy based on the "I don't much care where" philosophy of Alice. There should be a consistently positive sense of where we are going and how we plan to reach our destination. It means putting God first.

One writer suggests several ways to make God the number one priority in life. (1) Practice abiding in Him and being conscious of His presence moment by moment. (2) Spend time alone with Him every day. (3) Try seeking His presence for greater periods of time each day, week, month. (4) Go to church, "whether you feel like it or not, whether the preaching is great or isn't!"[10] Let Him direct your footsteps heavenward. Self-discipline wins goals. Winning brings a "crown that will last forever." 1 Corinthians 9:25, NIV. Only Christ can replace sadness with happiness and joy. Only He can fill your life with faith and hope when fear and anxiety seek to destroy you. He can blot out despair when the old, soul-destroying habits aren't easily overcome. Old habits die hard. Anyone who has tried to kill one off single-handedly will tell you that it can't be done. It is as difficult as pushing boulders uphill.

---

*empty, a shell, lacking substance, heartless.

The examples set by men and women who have gone before us awake an understanding of the responsibilities and potentialities which confront us today. Believers on this side of the cross need never suffer defeat. The universal prescription for happiness has always been found in total dedication to Christ. He alone can minimize conflicts and increase victories. He alone can mold the seemingly useless life into one that is rich and rewarding. Seventh-day Adventist Christians can be victorious in the home, in the church, and in the world. They possess the inspiration and confidence which motivate to service. They have become acutely aware of their role as trailblazers and goal setters, and they are prepared for the challenge this role offers. "Christian life is more than many take it to be. It does not consist wholly in gentleness, patience, meekness, and kindliness. These graces are essential; but there is need also of courage, force, energy, and perseverance. The path that Christ marks out is a narrow, self-denying path. To enter that path and press on through difficulties and discouragements require men [and women] who are more than weaklings."[11]

In 1924, some pertinent advice regarding politics was given which can be aptly applied to Christianity sixty years later— "Get into the game and stay in it. Throwing mud from the outside won't help. Building up from the inside will."[12] Get into the action and stay in it. Don't throw mud. (You can't help getting some on yourself. People who throw mud lose ground!) Construction not destruction. Spiritually, we are either growing or regressing; we are either helping to fortify the church (the body of Christ), or we are foolishly thinking we can destroy it. We are living on the Vine or dying because we have chosen to sever ourselves from Him. Build, erect, lift up Christ. Know where you stand and put your feet on the solid Rock. Encourage, don't discourage. "No discipline seems pleasant at the time, but painful. Later on, however, it produces a harvest of righteousness and peace for those who have been trained by it." Hebrews 12:11, NIV.

We need to make the world a better place while there is still time. We need to make the church, the community, the home a better place. We need to be doing, moving, growing. It is time to

dust off our creativity and get going. It is not enough to sit
around and think noble thoughts. We need workers who have
confidence and courage of conviction to stand boldly against as-
saults of prejudice. God wants His remnant church to push forward despite efforts to discourage and depress it. He needs
those who are in touch with Him in order to reach those who
are out of touch. He needs disciplined people who keep their
sights focused on the goal. At the end of the race, the crowns
and streets are made of gold. There is nothing wrong in looking
ahead to promised rewards. The best is yet to come.

Several years ago, I heard a group of talented musicians perform at camp meeting. I loved the grand old hymns and newer
gospel songs they played. As I listened, I wished I could do
something great like that for God. I pictured myself on stage
performing before vast audiences. There would be recording
contracts, gold records, and instant fame. I indulged in a good
old-fashioned ego trip. But of course, I would be humble about
all my talent. (Never mind that I have a hard time finding middle C on the piano.) When I finally settled back down to reality,
I realized that such fantasies are childish. Talents are devel-
oped, not just dreamed about and achieved overnight. The place
to concentrate is on the talents we already possess and to seek
to enlarge them to the best of our ability.

There is a bright light on the top of a mountain peak several
miles from downtown Palm Springs, California. It marks the
top of an aerial tram on San Jacinto Peak which takes visitors
from the valley floor to pine-studded vistas above. In the darkness, the light is visible for miles across the desert. It's just one
light in the middle of a wilderness. In the daylight, the most
distant object we can see is our sun, 93 million miles from
earth. At night, we can see stars and constellations which are
millions of light years away. Think of that the next time your
world turns black and you are tempted to think that your one
tiny light makes no difference.

Why do we dream and scheme and plan and plot to do something great for God *someday?* We look at talented musicians,
gifted professionals, and other popular people around us, and
we fantasize that *someday* we too will do something spectacular

for the Lord. In the meantime, the days grow shorter, and one morning we wake up to find that time has passed us by, because we were always waiting for the right opportunity or some magical moment (it would have to be miraculous) when we'd do something great for God.

Peter Marshall said, "Small deeds done are better than great deeds planned."[13] One tiny light in the midst of spiritual darkness can be seen by millions. God has promised that our little lights together shall light His world. Begin today by doing just one thing for God. Don't wait for another day to pass into history without setting a goal for yourself. Start now with one special project. Use the talents He has already given you; don't wish you had someone else's. Together, by His grace, we can do something wonderful. Never underestimate the power of one totally dedicated, Spirit-filled life. Look around you to find those in need. There is so much of hurting out there. Even if you can't talk, perhaps you can listen.

Tasks exist for God's people in the twentieth century as significant and compelling as any performed centuries ago. A new feeling of courage and hope, like a flower in the midst of a desert, has sprung up in our generation. We can choose to fill the hours with excuses, like waiting for the husband to retire or waiting for the children to grow up and leave home or waiting for someone else to change. Or we can change and choose to fill our days with productive, creative living, now. We can spend time in boring pursuits and unfulfilling projects, or we can spend our time in loving, caring, joy-filled service for others. We can occupy our years by merely existing, in trying to get by, in trying to stay young, in trying to gratify self, or we can fill them with trailblazing and achievement through Spirit-filled living. Time is precious; it is running out. Winners, overcomers, trailblazers do not waste it.

The old man in the window seat on Flight 1254 asked, "Where are you going?"

"Medford," I replied.

"Do you live there?"

"Yes. For fourteen years. How about you?"

"Yeh, for a hundred and fourteen!" He smiled and then

chuckled. As the plane began to climb, he shifted his position and stared out the window at the Golden Gate Bridge silhouetted against the shimmering waters of the Pacific. And then, with his gaze still fixed on the panoramic scene below, he said quietly, "My wife died of cancer four years ago."

It came without warning, like running into a brick wall in the darkness. It was startling. It jolted my mind. The open wound. The pain. The loneliness. Spilled out in heartwrenching words to a total stranger on a plane out of San Francisco.

I sat silently for a moment and then said, "I lost someone too. My father died of cancer."

He visibly relaxed and settled back into the seat. For the next hour, we talked about coping in life without someone we loved. About loneliness. About memories. Two strangers on a flight home, sharing thoughts and encouraging each other.

I have had similar experiences with people in waiting rooms, bus depots, and supermarket lines. From unknown faces beside me on the beach, in restaurants, at meetings. Lonely hearts reaching out to someone who will listen. It doesn't take a lot of talent to listen or care—just a heartfelt desire. The conversational pattern repeats itself again and again—"Hello. How are you? I hurt." The man on the flight home was no different. He typified the aching heart of humanity that surrounds us every day. After we had established the mutual bond of kinship that grief begets, he opened up the thoughts of his heart. The conversation overflowed as with an old friend. For a few bright, fleeting moments someone cared and filled an aching need— the ache of loneliness, the need for a friend.

The easiest choice to make in the hour of decision is to remain on the fence. It is so much easier to stay in the old, comfortable rut. But even a spiritual rut is no more than a grave with the ends kicked out. It will take true courage born through the realization of His direction in our lives in order for us to advance steadily with determination.

Ellen White sometimes autographed her books with the following paragraph:

"We are homeward bound. A little longer, and the strife will be over. May we who stand in the heat of the conflict, ever keep before us a vision of things unseen—of that time when the world in gladness will be bathed in the light of heaven, when the years will move on in gladness, when over the scene the morning stars will sing together and the sons of God will shout for joy, while God and Christ will unite in proclaiming, 'There shall be no more sin, neither shall there be any more death.' 'Forgetting those things which are behind, and reaching forth unto those things which are before,' let us 'press toward the mark for the prize of the high calling of God in Christ Jesus.' "[14]

One of my happiest childhood memories is of riding in our old Ford, with Dad and Mom in front, bumping along a dusty country road in Oregon. We were returning from camp meeting at Gladstone, and every few miles my brother or I would ask, "How far are we from home?" Partly due to exhaustion and partly out of childish impatience, we would ask that question over and over until we finally reached our destination.

At one time or another, I expect all of us have asked the same question, "How far to home?" After long vacations, weekend trips, or even a day out of town, no place is as welcome as home. No matter how humble the dwelling, its atmosphere is what we long for most. Familiar surroundings, loving and being loved, the happiness and closeness of family.

This brings to mind our heavenly home. Family, friends, and being with Jesus forever. Where the atmosphere is love, joy, and peace. Where we will never be separated again.

My father is gone now after a futile battle with cancer. His last words to Mother were, "I just want to go home." With an impatience born of longing, I just want to go home too. Home to be with Dad and Jesus. Surely we can't be far from home now.

"This is my prayer: that your love may abound more and more in knowledge and depth of insight, so that you may be able to discern what is best and may be pure and blameless until the day of Christ, filled with the fruit of righteousness that comes through Jesus Christ—to the glory and praise of God." Philippians 1:9-11, NIV.

References

CHAPTER HEADINGS

Chapter 1. Ellen G. White, *Testimonies for the Church* (Mountain View, Calif.: Pacific Press Publishing Association, 1948), vol. 4, p. 138.

Chapter 2. Amelia Barr, quoted in Elaine Partnow, compiler and editor, *The Quotable Woman: 1800-1975* (Los Angeles: Corwin Books, 1977), p. 62.

Chapter 3. Anne Morrow Lindbergh, *Gift From the Sea* (New York: Pantheon Books, 1955, 1975), p. 50.

Chapter 4. Ellen G. White, *Testimonies for the Church*, vol. 5, p. 168.

Chapter 5. Unknown author, quoted in Bruce Bohle, selector and arranger, *The Home Book of American Quotations* (New York: Dodd, Mead & Company, 1967), p. 289.

Chapter 6. Narcissa Prentiss Whitman in T. C. Elliott, compiler, *The Coming of the White Women, 1836* (Portland, Oreg.: Oregon Historical Society, 1937), p. [19].

Chapter 7. Nathaniel Hawthorne, *Twice-Told Tales* (New York: Dutton, n.d.), p. 319.

Chapter 8. Ellen G. White, *Testimonies for the Church*, vol. 3, p. 536.

Chapter 9. A. B. Simpson, quoted in Mrs. Charles E. Cowman, compiler, *Streams in the Desert* (Grand Rapids, Mich.: Zondervan Publishing House, 1925, 1965), p. 131.

CHAPTER 1: LOVE: Love's Kaleidoscope

1. June Strong, *A Little Journey* (Washington, D.C.: Review and Herald Publishing Association, 1984), p. 103.
2. Leo Buscaglia, *Love* (New York: Fawcett Crest, 1972), p. 84.
3. Ellen G. White, *Testimonies for the Church* (Mountain View, Calif.: Pacific Press Publishing Association, 1948), vol. 2, p. 169.
4. Ellen G. White, *Christ's Object Lessons* (Washington, D.C.: Review and Herald Publishing Association, 1941), p. 258.
5. Anne Ortlund, *Disciplines of the Beautiful Woman* (Waco, Tex.: Word Books, 1977), p. 26.
6. Ellen G. White, *The Adventist Home* (Nashville, Tenn.: Southern Publishing Association, 1952), p. 22.
7. Catherine Booth, quoted in Edith Deen, *Great Women of the Christian Faith* (New York: Harper & Brothers Publishers, 1959), p. 240.
8. Leonard Zunin, M.D. with Natalie Zunin, *Contact: The First Four Minutes* (New York: Ballantine Books, 1972), p. 1.
9. Helen Steiner Rice, "Yesterday . . . Today . . . and Tomorrow," quoted in Phyllis Hobe, ed., *Tapestries of Life* (Nashville, Tenn.: Holman Bible Publishers, 1974), p. 11.
10. Ellen G. White, *My Life Today* (Washington, D.C.: Review and Herald Publishing Association, 1952), p. 80.
11. Helen Keller, "My Luminous Universe," quoted in Norman Vincent Peale, ed., *Unlock Your Faith-Power* (Englewood Cliffs, N.J.: Prentice-Hall, Inc., 1957), p. 62.
12. R. D. Laing quoted in *Love* by Leo Buscaglia (New York: Fawcett Crest, 1972), p. 19.

CHAPTER 2: JOY: Joy Is an Inside Job

1. Eugenia Price, *Find Out for Yourself* (Grand Rapids, Mich.: Zondervan Publishing House, 1963), p. 158.
2. Douglas Cooper, *Living God's Joy* (Mountain View, Calif.: Pacific Press Publishing Association, 1979), p. 119.

CHAPTER 3: PEACE: Sanctuary of the Heart

1. Corrie ten Boom, *Tramp for the Lord* (Fort Washington, Penn.: Christian Literature Crusade and Old Tappan, N.J.: Fleming H. Revell Company, 1974), p. 30.

2. Ellen G. White, *Testimonies for the Church* (Mountain View, Calif.: Pacific Press Publishing Association, 1948), vol. 5, p. 488.

3. Phillip Keller, *A Shepherd Looks at Psalm 23* (Grand Rapids, Mich.: Zondervan Publishing House, 1970), p. 44.

4. Gordon Powell, *Happiness is a Habit* (Carmel, N.Y.: Guideposts Association, Inc., n.d.), p. 31.

5. Dr. Jeffrey Gould, quoted in "Fear of Nuclear War Among Young Common Worldwide." *Medford Mail Tribune*, December 9, 1984.

6. Eugene Kennedy, "Stress," quoted in *The Ann Landers Encyclopedia A to Z* (New York: Doubleday & Company, 1978), p. 1036.

7. Ellen G. White, *The Desire of Ages* (Mountain View, Calif.: Pacific Press Publishing Association, 1898, 1940), p. 525.

8. June Strong, *A Little Journey* (Washington, D.C.: Review and Herald Publishing Association, 1984), p. 124.

9. Ellen G. White, *Testimonies for the Church,* vol. 2, p. 196.

10. Anne Morrow Lindbergh, *Gift From the Sea* (New York: Pantheon Books, 1955, 1975), pp. 26, 27.

11. *Ibid.,* p. 16.

12. Margaret Blair Johnstone, "Ways to Find Your Secret Sanctuary," quoted in Norman Vincent Peale, ed., *Unlock Your Faith-Power* (Englewood Cliffs, N. J.: Prentice-Hall, Inc., 1957), p. 36.

13. Ellen G. White, *The Desire of Ages*, p. 90.

14. Ellen G. White, *Christ's Object Lessons* (Washington, D.C.: Review and Herald Publishing Association, 1941), pp. 174, 175.

15. Ellen G. White, *Messages to Young People* (Nashville, Tenn.: Southern Publishing Association, 1930), p. 250.

CHAPTER 4: PATIENCE: Saints Under Stress

1. Ellen G. White, *Testimonies for the Church* (Mountain View, Calif.: Pacific Press Publishing Association, 1948), vol. 3, p. 81.
2. Edith Deen, *All of the Women of the Bible* (New York: Harper and Brothers Publishers, 1955), pp. 109-112.
3. *The American College Dictionary* (New York: Wm. H. Wise & Co., Inc., 1952), p. 888.
4. Ellen G. White, *Testimonies for the Church,* vol. 7, p. 265.

CHAPTER 5: KINDNESS: Welcome As the Smiles of Angels

1. Ellen G. White, *Testimonies for the Church* (Mountain View, Calif.: Pacific Press Publishing Association, 1948), vol. 9, p. 189.
2. Dale Evans Rogers, *Hear the Children Crying* (Old Tappan, N.J.: Fleming H. Revell Company, 1978), p. 23.
3. Eugenia Price, *Woman to Woman* (Grand Rapids, Mich.: Zondervan Publishing House, 1959), p. 149.
4. Ellen G. White, *The Ministry of Healing* (Mountain View, Calif.: Pacific Press Publishing Association, 1905, 1909, 1937, 1942), p. 497.
5. Ellen G. White, *Testimonies for the Church,* vol. 5, p. 404.
6. Ellen G. White, *My Life Today* (Washington, D.C.: Review and Herald, 1952), p. 242.

CHAPTER 6: GOODNESS: Creative Living

1. Myron Eells, *Marcus Whitman: Pathfinder and Patriot* (Seattle, Wash.: Alice Harriman Company, 1909), p. 107.
2. Quoted in *The Women,* by the editors of Time-Life Books with text by Joan Swallow Reiter (Alexander, Va.: Time-Life Books, 1978), p. 24.
3. T. C. Elliott, compiler, *The Coming of the White Women, 1836* (Portland, Ore.: Oregon Historical Society, 1937), p. [84].
4. Marjorie Holmes, *Hold Me up a Little Longer, Lord* (Garden City, N. Y.: Doubleday & Company, Inc., 1977), p. 16.

5. Leslie Hardinge, "These Were Victors," *Adult Sabbath School Lessons*, no. 352, April-June 1983, p. 69.

6. *North Pacific Union Conference Gleaner,* May 16, 1983, p. 29.

7. Joan Macksey and Kenneth Macksey, *The Book of Women's Achievements* (New York: Stein and Day, 1975), pp. 107-110.

8. Gerry Peirce, "Creative You," quoted in Thomas S. Kepler, *Leaves From a Spiritual Notebook* (New York: Abingdon, 1960), p. 63.

9. Edward W. Bok, "You," quoted in Thomas S. Kepler, *Leaves From a Spiritual Notebook,* p. 61.

CHAPTER 7: FAITHFULNESS: Miry Pits and Spiritual Radar

1. Corrie ten Boom, *Tramp for the Lord* (Fort Washington, Penn.: Christian Literature Crusade and Old Tappan, N.J.: Fleming H. Revell Company, 1974), p. 12.

2. Joni Eareckson, "An Interview With Joni," *These Times,* November 1980, p. 12.

3. C. H. P., quoted in Mrs. Charles E. Cowman, compiler, *Streams in the Desert* (Grand Rapids, Mich.: Zondervan Publishing House, 1925, 1965), pp. 4, 5.

4. Ellen G. White, *Sons and Daughters of God* (Washington, D.C.: Review and Herald Publishing Association, 1955), p. 193.

5. Bronte Coffelt Smith, quoted in Charlotte L. Mahaffy, *Coos River Echoes* (Portland, Oreg.: Interstate Press, 1965), p. 147.

6. Ellen G. White, *Education* (Mountain View, Calif.: Pacific Press Publishing Association, 1903, 1952), p. 253.

7. Washington Irving, quoted in Phyllis Hobe, ed., *Tapestries of Life* (Nashville, Tenn.: Holman Bible Publishers, 1974), p. 184.

8. A. Graham Maxwell, *Can God Be Trusted?* (Nashville, Tenn.: Southern Publishing Association, 1977), p. 46.

CHAPTER 8: GENTLENESS: Dear Hearts and Gentle People

1. Ellen G. White, *Steps to Christ* (Mountain View, Calif.: Pacific Press Publishing Association, 1956), p. 100.

CHAPTER 9: SELF-CONTROL: Trailblazers and Goal Setters

1. Henry D. Thoreau, *The Annotated Walden,* ed. by Philip Van Doren Stern (New York: Clarkson N. Potter, Inc., Publisher, 1970), p. 168.

2. Edith Deen, *All of the Women of the Bible* (New York: Harper and Brothers Publishers, 1955), p. 23.

3. Ellen G. White, *The Acts of the Apostles* (Mountain View, Calif.: Pacific Press Publishing Association, 1911), pp. 560, 561.

4. Eugenia Price, *Woman to Woman* (Grand Rapids, Mich.: Zondervan Publishing House, 1959), p. 193.

5. *Ibid.,* p. 170.

6. Samuel Rutherford, quoted in Mrs. Charles E. Cowman, compiler, *Streams in the Desert* (Grand Rapids, Mich.: Zondervan Publishing House, 1925, 1965), p. 78.

7. Eleanor Roosevelt, *You Learn by Living* (New York: Harper & Brothers Publishers, 1960), p. 32.

8. Lewis Carroll, *Alice's Adventures in Wonderland,* in the chapter, "Pig and Pepper" (New York: Alfred A. Knopf, 1983), p. 72.

9. Robert Frost, "The Road Not Taken," in Edward Connery Lathem, ed., *The Poetry of Robert Frost* (New York: Holt, Rinehart and Winston, 1969), p. 105.

10. Anne Ortlund, *Disciplines of the Beautiful Woman* (Waco, Tex.: Word Books, 1977), p. 29.

11. Ellen G. White, *The Ministry of Healing* (Mountain View, Calif.: Pacific Press Publishing Association, 1905, 1909, 1937, 1942), p. 497.

12. Eleanor Roosevelt, quoted in Joseph P. Lash, *Eleanor and Franklin* (New York: W. W. Norton & Company, Inc., 1971), p. 288.

13. Peter Marshall, quoted in Phyllis Hobe, ed., *Tapestries of Life* (Nashville, Tenn.: Holman Bible Publishers, 1974), p. 14.

14. From my personal file.